MW01242801

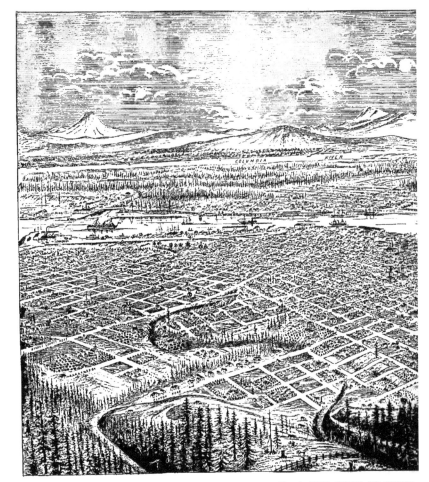

BIRD'S EYE VIEW OF PORTL:

Mt. Rainer (14,360 *feet*).   *Mt. Adams* (9,570 f

Mt. St. Helens (9,750 feet).

[Published by permission of Messrs. J. K. GILL & Co., P

GON.

Mt. Hood (11,025 *feet*).

of social and material development. Towns and cities had grown up, possessing all the elements of a stable prosperity. But the wide expanse of the interior country remained almost unknown. The broad lands of Eastern Oregon and Washington were the pasture grounds for immense herds and flocks—rich in cattle, sheep and horses, but poor in agricultural development and in population. Up to the summer of 1879, that wide region lying east of the Cascade Mountains was dependent for traveling and transportation facilities upon those supplied by a single company. This corporation owned the majority of steamboats on the Columbia and Willamette Rivers, and held possession of both sides of the great gorge of the Columbia River, where, by means of portage railroads, the steam-boat routes on the upper and lower waters of the stream were connected. Another railroad around The Dalles of the Columbia added to the security of the corporation, and still another narrow-gauge line from Wallula to Walla Walla, in Washington Territory, was owned by it. All the agricultural and other products of the rich region east of the Cascade Mountains were subject to handling and re-handling by the necessary transportation over this much broken route, and high freights were a most onerous tax upon the people.

It must be mentioned, also, that the Willamette Valley and the Umpqua Valley had already enjoyed a railroad epoch. Its result was a single road extending south two hundred miles to Roseburg, and afterwards another road on the west side of the Willamette Valley to the Yamhill river. But the credit of the State was seriously impaired by the financial failure of both these enterprises, and the prospect of continuing a railroad through to California was not cheering. Oregon stood as a bankrupt before railroad financiers, and the commerce of her vast interior was locked up in the embrace of a corporation that was content with large immediate profits, and was indifferent to the progress and development of the State. The whole region, indeed, was practically in a condition more despond-ing than expectant.

In the summer of 1879, the word was finally spoken which dispelled the dull-ness which had until then held sway, and an era of unexampled life and activity was begun. At this date, after strenuous and persistent effort, large capital was enlisted, the Oregon Railway and Navigation Company was organized, and, under the auspices of this company, great projects for developing the Pacific North-west have been successfully put into execution. First, the property and franchises of the Oregon Steam Navigation Company, and the steamship line to San Francisco, were secured by purchase. Soon afterwards active operations were entered upon to push branch roads to the great wheat-producing districts of the Upper Colum-bia river, and to construct a trunk line between Portland and the naturally rich interior.

The old steamers, between Portland and San Francisco, small wooden craft, uncomfortable and unseaworthy, were soon replaced by as fine iron steamships as float upon the ocean. The construction of a trunk railroad on the south bank of the Columbia river, from Walla Walla to Portland, was undertaken and has just been completed. From the latter place, the Northern Pacific Railroad is now building a line to Kalama, in order to make a through connection between Portland and the waters of Puget Sound. A fleet of fine steamships, owned by the Oregon Improvement Company, is developing the trade of all the ports on the coast, from Alaska to Southern California. The long-promised extension of the Oregon and

California Railroad, from its present terminus at Roseburg, to connect with a branch of the Central Pacific Railroad at the boundary line of Oregon and California. has been spurred on. The transportation facilities of the Willamette Valley have been greatly augmented by the operation of an extended line of narrow-gauge railroad in addition to the older railroads which traverse that valley. East of the Cascade Mountains, the Oregon Railway and Navigation Company has penetrated the very heart of the great wheat fields with fully-equipped standard-gauge railways, and is now rapidly extending its lines a total distance of several hundred miles. Indeed, in view of what this company has already accomplished, it virtually forms part of two leading trans-continental routes. It has been in connection for some time past with the Northern Pacific Railroad, near the confluence of the Columbia and Snake rivers, and its junction in the Grande Ronde Valley with the Oregon branch of the Union Pacific Railroad verges toward completion. Thousands of laborers are still in its employment, engaged in grading, tunneling, bridge-building and track-laying wherever production invites enterprise to build railroads, which, in many cases, will be the pioneers instead of the followers of settlement and civilization.

· The great results already attained can best be understood by the statement, that railroad construction has been pushed and steamboat routes extended until at present there are nearly 1,800 miles of transportation lines in operation, exclusive of 1,470 miles of ocean steamer navigation between San Francisco, Portland and the ports of Puget Sound. Before the close of 1883, there will probably be finished and in operation a grand aggregate of 6,000 miles of trunk lines and branches, all of which will meet in Portland. These lines will extend from St. Paul, in Minnesota, to Portland, to Puget Sound, and to San Francisco. They will, undoubtedly, give a wonderful impetus to the fertile regions of the Pacific Northwest by developing the unbounded resources of soil, forests and mines, and by putting to use the inexhaustible water power which now waits for man to claim and employ it. In view of all this, is it too much to assert that the time is at hand when not only population, but the capital necessary to the development of industries and manufactures, will flow into the Pacific North-west? Production has just begun. As soon as intercourse with the outer world shall be easily made by sea and land, the quarter of a million of inhabitants of 1880 will have swollen to half a million in 1885, and perhaps to one million in 1890.

The harvest year of 1880–81 gave the Columbia River ten million or more bushels of wheat to export, all of the best quality known to commerce. Within three years the shipments will probably reach twenty million bushels. Now eight to ten million pounds of wool are annually exported, and that, too, will increase proportionately. Coal and iron are in inexhaustible supply to build up prosperous industries. All that now is wanting is more brain, muscle and capital for the Pacific North-west to weave from the warp and woof of its destinies a great and wonderful future.

GEOGRAPHICAL AND HISTORICAL.

OREGON.

Oregon is situated between the parallels of 42' and 46° 18' north latitude, and between the meridians of 116° 33' and 124 25' west longitude from Greenwich. It is the most north-westerly State of the Union. On the north it is bounded by Washington Territory, the Columbia River forming the boundary to the point where that river crosses the parallel of 46° and the line running thence eastward along that parallel to the Snake River. Eastwardly it borders on Idaho Territory, the Snake River being the boundary to the mouth of the Owyhee, and thence by a line drawn due south along the meridian of 116° 05' west longitude to Nevada. On the south it is bounded by Nevada and California, the parallel of 42° north, forming the boundary line. The Pacific Ocean bounds it on the west.

The average width of Oregon from east to west is 350 miles, and from north to south 275 miles. Its full shore line is 285 miles. Its area is 95,274 square miles, or nearly 64,000,000 of acres. It is as large as all the New England States and two-thirds of the State of New York added to them, and larger than New York and Pennsylvania combined.

The population of the State, according to the official returns of the census of 1880, was 174,767, not quite two inhabitants to the square mile. The census of 1870 gave a population of 90,973, thus showing an increase of 83.794 in a single decade.

The discovery and exploration of Oregon and Washington Territory is credited to Spanish navigators early in the sixteenth century. It is also recorded that Juan de Fuca, a Greek mariner in the service of Mexico, sailed into Puget Sound in 1592. From time to time in the seventeenth century British and French navigators followed in the wake of the Spaniards. In 1792, Captain Robert Gray, of Boston, commanding the ship Columbia, discovered and sailed up the river which now bears the name of his vessel. Upon this discovery and exploration of Captain Gray, the United States subsequently based its claim to the region now embraced by Oregon and Washington Territory, which was formally ceded to this country by Spain under the treaty of Florida, concluded in 1819.

In 1804, an overland expedition under Captains Lewis and Clark, U. S. Army, crossed the Rocky Mountains, and having followed the Columbia River from its head waters, reached Cape Disappointment in November, 1805. The valuable resources of the Pacific coast were first made known by this expedition.

In 1810, the first attempt at a settlement was made in Oregon at Oak Point, on the south side of the Columbia River, by Captain Nathaniel Winship, a New England sailor. A freshet soon after carried away the buildings and the enterprise was abandoned.

In 1811, a trading post was established by John Jacob Astor, of New York, at the mouth of the Columbia River, and the place was called "Astoria," in his honor. Chiefly in consequence of the war of 1812 between the United States and Great Britain this venture proved disastrous. In 1813, the British took possession of the post and named it Fort George. The Hudson Bay Company subsequently obtained the property, ruling supremely in the valleys of the Columbia and the Willamette-until 1848, excepting, however, a few years prior to 1824, when its sway was disputed for a time by the North-west Fur Company, which latter corporation was compelled to yield to its stronger competitor.

In 1824, the first fruit trees were planted in Oregon. In 1831, some servants of the Hudson Bay Company abandoned hunting and trapping and attempted wheat growing in the Willamette valley. The fields then ploughed have been in constant cultivation ever since, and, after the lapse of half a century, one of them at French Prairie, Marion County, still yielded, in 1879, thirty-five bushels to the acre. This, indeed, must be superior soil, and the fact is a striking illustration of the strength and productiveness of the land. In 1832, the first school was opened. Between 1835 and 1837, missions were established under the auspices of various religious societies and denominations, and the missionaries brought cattle with them. In 1838, the first printing press arrived in Oregon.

In 1841, Captain Wilkes, U. S. Navy, at the head of an expedition, surveyed the coasts, bays, harbors and rivers of the territory. In 1843, Lieut. Fremont, U. S. Army, reached Vancouver, on the Columbia River, and so connected his reconnoissance with the eastern terminus of Captain Wilkes's explorations.

The territory was the subject of repeated negotiations and threatening controversies between the United States and Great Britain from 1813 to 1846. In the last named year a treaty was signed by the contending powers which fixed 49° north latitude as the northern boundary of the claim of the United States. Meanwhile, since 1841, there had been considerable increase in the American population, settlers chiefly coming from the border slave States ; until, at the time of the cession, the whites numbered about ten thousand. But during all the years in which supremacy over the territory remained unsettled, the country was held in joint occupancy by both nations, under conventions which were from time to time renewed. Nevertheless, no form of civil government existed. In 1845, the inhabitants had already found themselves compelled to adopt a provisional government, and this continued in force until 1848. In this year Oregon Territory was organized by Congress, and in 1849 General Joseph Lane was appointed Governor. By the seventh census of the United States, in 1850, it appeared that the territory embraced 308,052 square miles and had 13,294 inhabitants. At this date, also, Vancouver was the headquarters of the immense trade of the Hudson Bay Company. Subsequently the Territories of Washington and northern Idaho and Montana, west of the Rocky Mountains, were partitioned from it.

In 1846, the first newspaper was established. In the succeeding year a massacre of settlers by the Indians occurred. This was the beginning of much subsequent trouble with the aborigines which retarded the development of the country to a great extent. Indian difficulties, however, have happily ceased in recent years, and the Indians are now quietly situated on reservations where they are provided for and educated.

In 1859, Oregon was admitted into the Union as a State, with a population of 52,465 souls. Her progress for many years thereafter was comparatively slow. The chief difficulty which her people encountered was to find a market for her abundant agricultural productions. But this serious obstacle to her rapid advancement has been surmounted, as already explained, by affording the proper means of railroad transportation

NORTHERN PACIFIC RAILROAD AND OREGON RAILWAY AND
NAVIGATION COMPANY'S OFFICES, PORTLAND, OREGON.

WASHINGTON TERRITORY.

Before Alaska, which is not yet organized, was added to the domain of the United States, the most north-western part of the country was Washington Territory. This Territory lies between the parallels 45° 32' and 49° north latitude, and the meridians of 117° and 124° 8' west longitude from Greenwich. On the west it is bounded by the Pacific Ocean. On the north it is divided from British Columbia by a line running through the centre of the Strait of Juan de Fuca, the Canal de Haro and the Gulf of Georgia as far as the 49th parallel; thence along this parallel to the west line of Idaho. This northern line is, therefore, quite uneven. It was run so crookedly, after a tedious arbitration, in order that Great Britain might not be deprived of important settlements which her subjects mainly occupied. In reality, the claim of the United States was valid to all the territory south of the 49th parallel to the Pacific Ocean. But a strict enforcement of this title would have taken in nearly all of Vancouver's Island, where numbers of British colonists dwelt. On the south, the Columbia River, to about the 119th meridian, and thence, eastwardly, the 46th parallel, separate the Territory from Oregon. Its limit on the east is Idaho along the 117th meridian to Lewiston, and then the line follows the Snake River till it intersects with that of Oregon.

The length of Washington Territory, from north to south, ranges from 200 to 250 miles, and its greatest breadth from east to west is about 360 miles. Its coast length is 245 miles, and its full shore line 1,738 miles. It is smaller than most of the Territories and several of the Western States, having an area only of 69,994 square miles, or 44,796,160 acres, but is, nevertheless, one-and-a-half times as large as New York or Pennsylvania. Exclusive of the area covered by the waters of Puget Sound, and the mountainous region, which are unfit for cultivation, there would probably remain 35,000,000 acres. Of these 20,000,000 acres are timber lands, about 5,000,000 are rich alluvial bottoms, and 10,000,000 are prairies and plains. Of the latter, a large proportion is well adapted for wheat culture, and all of it for stock raising.

The tenth census of the United States, taken in 1880, gave the Territory 75,120 inhabitants, or about one to the square mile.

The history of Washington Territory, until 1853, when Congress endowed it with separate political life and conferred upon it a name and identity, is closely allied with that of Oregon. At the date of organization it contained only 3,965 white inhabitants, of whom 1,682 were voters. Its first Governor was Major Isaac I. Stevens, U. S. Engineers, who subsequently fell in the civil war as a General in the army of the Union. Olympia, pleasantly situated at the head of Puget Sound, was selected as the capital, and the first Territorial Legislature convened there in 1854. The Western portion of the Territory, especially the region of Puget Sound, was always a favorite habitat of the Indians. Indians. In 1840, there were not less than 25,000 Indians dwelling there, who found existence easy on account of the abundance of game and fish. From time to time there were difficulties with the aborigines in various parts of the Territory, until in November, 1855, a general outbreak occurred, preceded by a massacre of settlers on White River, on the shores of Puget Sound, and the frequent murder of individuals and small parties on their way to and from the Colville mines. The Indian war, known as the "Oregon-Washington Indian War," was the result of these repeated outrages. It raged violently from the autumn of 1855, to mid-summer, 1856, before the Indians were forced to succumb. This war was entirely unprovoked by the people of the Territory. It was simply waged by them in defence of the right of settlement. Subsequently there were occasional troubles, but not in very recent years. In the whole Territory there are now about 14,000 Indians, who are domiciled at various reservations, where they live peaceably and are gradually advancing in civilization. In 1858-9, there was a great accession to the population in consequent of the discovery of gold on the Frazer River, British Columbia, in the preceding year. Large numbers of people flocked into the Territory in 1861-2, during the time of excitement incident to the gold discoveries on the Salmon River. In 1863, the Territory of Idaho was taken off from Washington, and the area of the latter was thus reduced to one-half its former limits. During recent years there has been a constantly increasing development of the varied and abounding natural resources of the Territory. Farming, mining, lumbering and fishing offer infinite opportunities for the successful display of enterprise and energy.

TOPOGRAPHICAL.

MOUNTAINS.

The Cascade Mountains, which take their name from the numerous waterfalls that pour down their rugged faces, divide the entire Territory into two unequal parts, each of which is characterized by a marked dissimilarity in topography, soil, climate and, to some extent, productions. This range of mountains is a prolongation of the Sierra Nevada chain, and traverses Oregon and Washington in a course slightly deviating from north and south. The average distance of these mountains from the Pacific Ocean is about 110 miles. As the range reaches northward it puts out spurs in many directions, so that the whole country west of the Columbia is broken and hilly. Snow-capped peaks of grand proportions and sublime aspect are a striking feature in the landscape. Their summits and ridges are covered with everlasting snow, which makes them visible at great distances, appearing sometimes like summer clouds of fleecy whiteness, and at others bathed in brilliant lights. The most elevated peaks are Mount Rainier (14,360 feet), Mount Baker (11,100 feet), Mount Hood (11,025 feet), Mount St. Helens (9,750 feet), and Mount Adams (9,570 feet).

At a distance, varying from forty to seventy miles west of the Cascade Mountains, is another mountain chain, running also north and south, known as the Coast Range. Generally separated from the Pacific Ocean by an intervening narrow strip of upland, this range has an altitude of from three to five thousand feet, with the exception of the principal peak, called Mount Olympus, not far distant from Puget Sound, which towers to the height of eight thousand feet. These mountains are all densely wooded, and offer many passes through which the sea fogs roll and the ocean winds rush.

About 150 miles east of the Cascade Mountains, the Blue Mountains stretch in a general north-east and south-west direction through the country. Still another mountain range known as the "Western Spur" of the Blue Mountains extends at right angles with the main chain, in a course from north-west to south-east, from the mouth of Trout Creek, on the Dés Chutes River, to the Malheur River. A parallel but shorter chain runs from Camp Curry to Crooked Lake.

These mountain ranges, conjointly with the numerous hills which flank and border and run out from them, especially in the country west of the Cascade Mountains, break and disrupt the surface of the land, bisecting it into numberless valleys of varying extent and of great fertility, each of which is traversed by a more or less important stream. The scenic beauty of the whole vast region is, indeed, marvelous, and it can scarcely be surpassed in the diversity of its charms by any other portion of the United States.

RIVERS, HARBORS, ETC.

The largest river of the Pacific North-west is the Columbia. This mighty stream, with its numerous affluents, drains an area of 395,000 square miles. Rising in the Rocky Mountains in latitude 50° 20′ N., it flows northward to 52° 10′. Receiving Canoe River, which has its source in 53° N., it abruptly turns south-ward, expanding in 51° into a chain of small lakes, the Kootenai River uniting with it in 49° 30′ N. Immediately south of 49° the great north branch of the Columbia, known as Clark's Fork, pours its waters into the main stream through Lake Pend d'Oreille. Then flowing south, the Columbia receives the Spokane, after which it turns almost due west, and is joined by the Okanagane from the north. The river now follows a course south of west, and the Methow, the Chelan, the Entcatwa, and the Wenachee contribute to its volume. Then turning south-eastwardly the Yakima unites with it. Afterwards, it receives the waters of Snake River (formerly Lewis' Fork), its great southern branch. Flowing south-ward, the Walla Walla empties into it at about 46° N., then sharply turning west, it takes in the waters of the Umatilla, the John Day and the Des Chutes. The Columbia now forces its way at The Dalles through a narrow gorge in the Cascade Mountains, and afterwards receives the Klikitat, the Hood, the White Salmon, the Wind and other rivers. One hundred miles from the mouth of the Columbia, its largest tributary, the Willamette River, empties into it, and in the remainder of its course to the Pacific Ocean it receives the flow from the Lewis, the Cowlitz and the Young Rivers, as well as other less important streams. The Columbia River and its tributaries penetrate in every direction through the length and breadth of twelve degrees of latitude and thirteen of longitude. The great value of this stream as a means of transportation is apparent when it is considered that the distance between its navigable waters and the Missouri River is only 450 miles. Excluding the portages at the Cascades, at The Dalles, at Priest's and Buckland's Rapids, and at the mouth of the Methow, the river is navigable to Kettle Falls, a distance of 725 miles from its mouth. From that point it could be navigated still further for 150 miles into the heart of the richest mining regions of British Colum-bia. At the Cascades, where, in the length of four miles, the river falls a distance of 300 feet, the United States Government is constructing a series of locks, which will assist navigation materially as soon as they are finished.

SNAKE RIVER.—The source of the Snake River is in 41° N., and 111° W. It is one of the largest affluents of the Columbia, and its main tributaries are the

Grande Ronde, the Powder, the Burnt, the Malheur, and the Owyhee Rivers. From its confluence, at Ainsworth, with the Columbia, it is navigable to Lewiston, in Idaho, a distance of over 150 miles.

WILLAMETTE RIVER.—This important stream rises in the Cascade Mountains, and with the exception of the Columbia, is the chief river in Oregon. The Willamette is formed by the three streams known as McKenzie's, Middle and Coast Forks. It is navigable for the largest ocean steamships and sailing vessels to Portland, 112 miles from the sea. At Oregon City it falls perpendicularly over a ledge of rocks about 40 feet high. Formerly these falls proved an absolute obstruction to direct navigation, and a passage around them was secured by a portage on the right bank of the river. Subsequently, at a cost of several hundred thousand dollars, locks were constructed, allowing the direct passage of steamboats. Now these vessels navigate the river during high water as far as Eugene City, 188 miles from Portland, and as far as Salem, 51 miles, during the whole year. Small steamers of very light draught have been recently introduced in order that the river may be navigated uninterruptedly at every season. The main tributaries of the Willamette are the Tualatin, the Clackamas, the Yamhill, the Mollala, the Santiam, the Luckiamute, the Mary and the Long Tom Rivers.

OTHER RIVERS.—The largest rivers which empty into the Pacific Ocean along the coast of Oregon are the Rogue, the Coquille, the Umpqua, the Siuslaw, the Alsea, the Siletz and the Nehalem. North of the entrance to the Columbia River, on the coast of Washington Territory, the rivers Talux, Nasal and Willopah flow into Shoalwater Bay, and the Chehalis River and other streams empty into Gray's Harbor. Thirty-eight miles south of Cape Flattery the Quillyhuyte River flows into the Pacific Ocean. Most of these rivers are navigable for long distances and beside them are very many more which afford passage for vessels of light draft.

PUGET SOUND REGION.—This great body of tide-water, often called the Mediterranean of America, covers an area within Washington Territory of over 2,000 square miles, and has a shore line of 1,800 miles. It is a beautiful archipelago, extending from the British line on the north, embracing the Straits of San Juan de Fuca, which afford a broad and absolutely unobstructed channel to the ocean, the Gulf of Georgia, which reaches several hundred miles into British Columbia, the Canal de Haro, Bellingham Bay, Rosario Straits, Possession Sound, Admiralty Inlet, Hood's Canal and other passes and inlets. Its waters are everywhere deep and free from shoals ; the shores of its bays and harbors are bold ; its anchorage is land-locked and secure, and it offers, in fine, every facility which the necessities of a great commerce would demand. Its more commodious harbors are Neah Bay, Port Discovery, Port Townsend, Port Ludlow, Port Madison, Port Gamble, Port Orchard, Port Blakely, Elliot's Bay, upon which the thriving City of Seattle is situated, Commencement Bay, Tacoma, Steilacoom, Budd's Inlet, on which lies Olympia, the capital of the Territory, Tulalip, Penn's Cove, Utsalada, and Bellingham. At each of these places towns already exist or extensive lumbering and mining enterprises are carried on

The rivers emptying into Puget Sound are the Lummi, the Nooksahk, the Swinamish, the Skagit, the Snohomish, the Skywamish, the Suoqualmie, the Dwamish, the Puyallup, the Nisqually, the Des Chutes, the Skokomish, the Dungeness, the Elwha and several smaller streams. These rivers afford many hundred miles of inland navigation for steamers of light draft and for logging

NEW-TACOMA, PUGET SOUND, W. T.

(*Terminus Pacific Division of Northern Pacific Railroad.*)

purposes. The valleys of these streams, with those of their affluents, have an estimated area of 2,000 square miles of alluvial agricultural lands. Water-power sites are quite abundant, and gold is found in paying quantities in many of the river beds. The whole region is inexhaustibly rich in timber, as well as in deposits of coal and iron.

LAKES.—In addition to the water-courses, there are in Oregon and Washington many lakes, some of which are of considerable size and importance. Among these may be named Klamath, Goose, Warner and Harney Lakes in Oregon, and Chelann, Kahchess, Washington and Whatcom in Washington Territory.

BAYS AND HARBORS.—On the coast line there are several commodious harbors for vessels of light draft, exclusive of those at the mouths of the several rivers. Of these harbors the principal are to be found at Coos, Yaquina and Tillamook Bays in Oregon, and Shoalwater Bay, Gray's Harbor and Bellingham Bay in Washington. At each of these places there is a thriving trade prosecuted either in lumbering, coal mining, fishing, oystering, dairying and in the products of agriculture.

VALLEYS.

The great mountain chains and the smaller ranges which stretch out from them create numberless valleys in the Pacific North-west, which give the country a distinctive character. The Cascade Mountains divide the region into two colossal basins. East of them, and extending to the bases of the Blue and Bitter Root ranges, stretches out the broad rolling plateau of the Columbia River, covering an area 150 miles wide by nearly 500 long, and embracing within its limits a score of valleys, many a one of which is larger than some European principalities. West of the Cascade Mountains and lying between them and the Coast Range, spreads out another grand basin, nearly four hundred miles in length, and seventy-five in breadth, which is broken up into a series of valleys, some of which are extremely large. Included in the latter division are the great valleys of the Willamette, the Rogue, and the Umpqua Rivers, in Oregon, and the Chehalis Valley in Washington Territory. The principal valleys east of the Cascade Mountains are the Klamath, the John Day, the Umatilla, the Walla Walla, the Grande Ronde, the Powder River, the Jordan River, the Touchet, the Tuckannon, the Palouse, the Yakima and the Spokane.

CLIMATE.

An erroneous opinion as to the climate of the Northern Pacific coast is widely current in the Eastern States. Usually Oregon and Washington are associated in the public mind with a region of rigorous and prolonged winters. But the fact is quite the reverse. The severe winters and sultry summers and all the capricious inequalities of temperature prevalent in the States on the same parallels of latitude eastward of the Rocky Mountains are not known. The mildness and equability of the climate resembles in these respects that of Western Europe. It is genial and steady, offering the golden mean between the heat that debilitates and the cold that benumbs. The fact is well attested that on the Pacific Slope of the Rocky Mountains, north of 32° of latitude, the isothermal lines generally run north-west and south-east, and not east and west as they do on the Atlantic declivities. The mean temperature of January ranges from 10˚ to 20 higher, according to locality, on the Pacific side than it does on the Atlantic side of this mountain chain which partitions the continent. This difference in the temperature of the two divisions is caused by the Kurosiwo or Japan current, which modifies the climate of the North Pacific coast in the same manner that the Gulf Stream, flowing across the North Atlantic ocean, tempers the climate of the British Isles.

But this general statement requires explanation. There is a great dissimilarity in the climate of Oregon and Washington between those lands lying west of the Cascade Mountains and the immense plains and undulating prairies which lie east of this range.

West of the Cascade Mountains the winters are rainy rather than cold. The range of temperature demonstrates this fact. The average for spring is 52˚; for summer 67˚; for autumn 53˚, and for winter 38˚, showing a mean deviation of only 28 during the year. The winter, or rainy season, begins about the middle of October, often later, and ends about the first of May. The rains are more copious in December, January and March than at any other time. During many weeks at the beginning and toward the close of the wet season, the rain falls rather in showers than continuously, with many intervals of bright, agreeable weather which often last for days together. Snow sometimes falls during the winter months, but rarely in great quantities, and it soon disappears under the influence of the humid atmosphere. This region is almost exempt from violent atmospheric disturbances. Thunder storms seldom occur, and hailstorms, hurricanes, whirlwinds, earthquakes and other destructive phenomena are all but unknown. The comparative freedom of this country from high winds is shown by the wind-records, kept by the United States Government, and extending over a period of twenty-seven years.

In Western Oregon and Washington Territory, whenever the thermometer falls a few degrees below the freezing-point, the weather is usually bright and pleasant, with heavy white frosts at night. When frosts occur during spring or early summer, which in other lands would be sufficiently severe to injure fruit and growing crops, they are commonly followed by heavy fogs, which roll in from the ocean and spread themselves throughout the country. These fogs are so very dense that their humidity dissolves the frost before the heat of the sun can strike the vegetation. Consequently, within the area of these foggy belts, the late frosts do no harm to vegetation. On the ocean faces of the coast range the grass is kept perennially green by the moist atmosphere, and this is the case almost everywhere else in the low-lying lands. Indeed, it is not unusual for flowers to bloom in the open air the winter through.

Only in very exceptional years is ice formed sufficiently thick that it may be cut for use, and skating is a pastime in which youth rarely have an opportunity to engage. The mild spring opens so early that the farmer sows his seed, the apple, pear and cherry trees are in bloom, and the children gather wild flowers in the meadows at a time when, in latitude from four to six degrees further south on the Atlantic coast, the rigors of winter are still unrelaxed.

During the remainder of the year, the long interval between the middle of October and April, the weather, as a rule, is serene and delightful. Throughout this period there are showers from time to time, but the face of the country is kept fresh and verdant by the dews of night and occasional fogs in the morning. The extreme dry season begins in July, but even the warmest summer days are tempered by sea-breezes and followed by cool nights. The coldest hours of the summer evenings are between 9 and 11 o'clock, but towards morning the temperature rises.

It must be borne in mind that the climate of the country east of the Cascade Mountains has characteristics widely differing from that of the great basin lying west of them already described. This is not only true of climate, but also with respect to soil and natural features. The popular division of the country, therefore, by the Cascade Range into two sections, known respectively as Eastern and Western Oregon and Washington Territory, is warranted.

In Eastern Oregon and Washington Territory, by far the larger area, the temperature is much lower in winter and higher in summer than it is west of the mountain barrier. The rainfall is also not one-half as heavy. In all this region, which may be termed, generically, the great valley of the Columbia River, the summers are often very hot. The thermometer not infrequently reaches 95°, and between 80° and 90° is the ordinary temperature. This heat, however, is not sultry nor nearly so oppressive as a much lower grade would be in the Eastern States, both man and beast being able to labor on the hottest days without special inconvenience. The nights are invariably cool and refreshing, and make light blankets a necessary part of the bed clothing. During this season there is absolutely no rain from June to September, thus giving the farmer perfect weather for harvesting and threshing his grain.

The winters, as a rule, are short, but occasionally severe. Exceptionally, the thermometer sinks to zero, and sometimes even a few degrees lower, but 30° is about the average temperature. Snow seldom falls before Christmas, and then, in some seasons, it may lie a month or six weeks. Usually, however, it disappears within a few days. The speedy melting of the snow is due, at times, to a somewhat remarkable phenomenon. A periodical warm wind blows up the channel of the Columbia River from the south-west throughout the year. This is called the "Chinook." It penetrates the gaps and passes of the mountain ranges as far east as Montana. Before it the snow melts so rapidly that often in the course of a few hours no vestige remains where it lay a foot in depth a day before. The "Chinook" wind is a great benefit to the country. Its warm, moist atmosphere is doubtless the result of its passage across the great thermal ocean stream, known as the Japan current, which operates so powerfully to mitigate the climate of the entire North-west Coast, that otherwise would be cold and rigorous in the extreme.

Spring begins in February with warm, pleasant weather, and lasts until the middle of May. At this season rain falls in sufficient quantity to give life to vegetation and insure good crops. The average temperature is 52°.

Autumn weather in October and November is generally delightful. There is often frost by night, but the days are usually warm and bright. The season is marked by showers, and also by thunder storms in some localities. The mercury ranges between 55° and 70°.

The rainfall of the year does not average more than 20 inches. South of the Snake River it is not more than 15 inches, increasing gradually to the northward.*

---

* See Tables in the Appendix.

The foregoing description of the climate of Oregon and Washington Territory must be understood, however, as applicable only to the general meteorological characteristics of the two grand divisions of the country. These characteristics are naturally modified to a greater or less extent by locality. The region is vast enough to embrace much variety of climate within the broad limits of the facts here presented. Intending settlers thus have a wide range of climate from which to choose that which may appear to them most desirable. Indeed, the truth with respect to the climate and fertility of the Pacific North-west is so at variance with preconceived ideas that it is hardly possible to state the facts without seeming to exaggerate.

The railroad lands are sold to settlers at low prices and on eas

THE SOIL.

The excellence of the soil of Oregon and Washington Territory is not less marked than that of the climate. The combination of good climate and fruitful soil gives the country its exceptional value for agricultural pursuits.

In Western Oregon and Washington the general character of the soil may be described as follows: In the valleys it is a dark loam containing a large proportion of vegetable mould and having a clay sub-soil. In the bottom-lands, near the water-courses, it usually consists of rich deposits of alluvium. Of such lands there are often large tracts of great fertility, termed beaver-dam lands, which, as the name indicates, have been formed by the labor of this busy amphibious rodent during countless centuries. The constituents of this soil are earthy deposits or humus of great depth, produced from decayed trees and other vegetable growths. All these various soils are of wonderful productive capacity. Under cultivation they are quick, light and friable, yielding astonishing crops of hay, hops, grain, fruits and vegetables for a series of years, without manure and with only indifferent ploughing. The ability of the clay sub-soil to retain moisture explains, to some extent, the enduring quality of the land. The bottoms are mainly covered with a deciduous growth of vine-maple, alder, crab-apple and salal-berry, with only occasional firs and pines, and, as a rule, are confined to narrow valleys. Unlike prairie-lands, they must be cleared, at a cost varying from $15 to $20 per acre, before they can be ploughed. Usually, however, the wood and lumber thus secured will pay for the work, and the farmer will afterwards find his reward in the abundance of his crops.

The soil of the uplands is somewhat inferior to that of the river-bottoms. That of the undulating foot-hills and more tillable mountain-faces is red, brown or black loam. The more elevated lands afford excellent natural pasturage, and also produce good crops of grain and the hardier fruits and vegetables.

East of the Cascade Mountains, the soil is a dark loam of great depth, composed of alluvial deposits and decomposed lava overlying a clay sub-soil. This, in turn, rests upon a basaltic formation which is so far below the surface of the ground as to be visible only on the banks of the deep water-courses. The constituents of this soil adapt the land peculiarly to the production of wheat. All the mineral salts which are necessary to the perfect growth of this cereal are abundant, reproducing themselves constantly as the processes of gradual decomposition in this soil of volcanic origin proceed. The clods are easily broken by the plough, and the ground quickly crumbles on exposure to the atmosphere. Although the dry season continues for months, this light porous land retains and absorbs enough moisture from the atmosphere, after its particles have been partially disintegrated, to insure perfect growths and full harvests. This assertion is so at variance with common experience that it might well be questioned. Happily, it is susceptible of explanation. In spite of the fact that there is scarcely a shower between May and the following October, and that the average rainfall for the year does not exceed 20 inches, there is always the requisite moisture for maturing the crops. Paradoxical as it may seem, if the rain were greatly in excess of this low average, damage would certainly ensue ; and it is equally sure, if successful farming depended upon the limited rainfall, there would be poor harvests. The clouds supply only in part the moisture which is needed. The warm air-currents, surcharged with vapor, which sweep inland from the ocean up the channel of the Columbia River, prevent drought. The effect of these atmospheric currents in tempering the climate has already been described. Their influence upon the vegetation is no less vital. The moisture with which they are laden is held in suspension during the day, diffused over the face of the country. At night it is condensed by the cooler temperature and precipitated in the form of a fine mist on every exposed particle of surface which earth and plant present. The effect is that of a copious shower. This is apparent on taking a morning walk through the grass, which can only be done at the cost of wet feet. In this region it is no unusual phenomenon for a smart shower to fall when clouds are invisible and the sun is shining. This occurrence is explained also upon the theory that the vapor in the atmosphere comes in contact with an upper current of cold air, which causes rapid condensation and consequent rain. A summer drought, therefore, which in most climates is a calamity, is here a benefit. The soil needs no more rains after those of the spring are over, and the farmer may depend upon cloudless skies at harvest time. In the whole vast basin of the Columbia River, an extent of 150 miles in width by 500 in length, there is great uniformity in the general character of the arable soil. There are, of course, modifications of its component elements, as between the valleys and the higher plateaux and lower mountain slopes. In the latter an admixture of clay to some extent is often found. In general, the soil of the foot-hills is more productive than that of the broader valleys.

The exceeding fertility of this great area has only of late years been known. Some of the large wheat farms, which now are most productive, were marked not long ago upon the maps, by the United States surveyors, as " lands unfit for cultivation." The prolific nature of the soil was discovered, finally, by a thoughtful investigator, who ploughed and sowed a small strip as an experiment. The result was a surprise and a success. It at once opened the way to the profitable cultivation of the hitherto despised land. Now, wherever bunch-grass grows, the fact is accepted that wheat will flourish. Of such lands there are almost boundless tracts awaiting settlement. A mere fraction of the vast fields has yet been taken. In course of time, however, these unoccupied lands will be surveyed and settled, depending on the facilities which may be offered by transportation lines for marketing crops. For the most part, these vast expanses of good, arable soil are the grazing grounds of countless herds and flocks, which thrive, unsheltered, the year throughout, on the natural grasses, and supply with their increase the markets of

Utah, Nevada and other States. Even the white sage bush, when its leaves have been mellowed by the frost, is relished by the cattle.

Most of the fruits grown within the temperate zone are raised at various points in the low-lying lands in great perfection. Peaches, pears, apples, plums, grapes and berries of fine flavor are produced. Orchards come forward rapidly, peach trees bearing often three years after planting the seed.

The greatest difficulty which the settler will encounter in taking up a farm in any of these great arable tracts, is the comparative absence of timber. There are groves of cottonwood, birch, alder and willow along the water-courses, but pine, fir and tamarack must be transported as a general fact from the mountains. Numerous mills have been established in the hills, and, in many instances, these are connected to railroad stations with flumes which transport the lumber to central points for distribution. The cost of lumber at the mills is about $12 per thousand feet, and at the yards it ranges to a much higher figure, according to the distance it has to be transported.

HEATHFULNESS.

The temperate and genial climate, especially in its freedom from the sudden variations which prevail elsewhere, has much to do with the general healthfulness of the Pacific North-west. According to the census of 1870, this part of the United States was by far the most healthy. Although twelve years have since passed, it will probably be found that Oregon and Washington Territory still bear the palm. Naturally the health of the different districts varies in accordance with location. Portland, the metropolis of Oregon and of the whole region, is remarkably healthy, having, of course, its quota of diseases. The complaints incidental to childhood prevail seldom as severe epidemics. Scarlet fever, as a rule, is not of a malignant type, and the percentage of deaths is smaller than in the cities of the Atlantic coast. Occasional cases of diphtheria occur, though never in an epidemic form, the causes elsewhere prevailing being there absent. The climate of the city and of the western slope of the Cascade Mountains is not suitable for individuals suffering from phthisis or other diseases of the lungs, and is also ill adapted to those of a rheumatic tendency, because of the moisture and excessive rains of the winter season. Typhoid fever appears, as elsewhere, as well as other ordinary diseases. Typhus fever never occurs. Cholera, which has been a scourge in the East, has never reached this part of the Pacific coast. The inhabitants of towns situated on the banks of the rivers suffer more or less from malaria, as is the case elsewhere in places so situated. The further back one goes from the coast, the air is found to be more rarefied, and in some respects more healthy. Those who have a tendency to diseases of the respiratory organs in many cases recover their health by a residence at The Dalles, Walla Walla and other places in Eastern Oregon and Washington. Mineral springs have been discovered which, in time, will attract great attention.

In summing up the answer to the inquiry of those contemplating settlement, as to the health of the country and the prevailing diseases, it may be said that all, or nearly all, the ordinary diseases occur. There are none, however, peculiar to the country. Moreover, as a rule, those prevalent elsewhere are found to be of a milder type in Oregon and Washington, and consequently less dreaded. Many diseases become malignant and destructive in crowded neighborhoods because the flame is constantly fed by the germs of the disease, which are continually generated and are easily spread from one person to another. But where, as in the Pacific North-west, there is no need of crowding, almost every disease soon dies out because it fails to obtain nourishment. On logical ground it may be assumed, therefore, apart from the question of climate, that the people of Oregon and Washington Territory will enjoy great longevity, and that the country will remain healthy simply because artificial causes of disease are absent.

PRODUCTIONS.

CEREALS, VEGETABLES, FRUIT AND OTHER CROPS.

Wheat is the staple agricultural product of the entire country. Its superior quality has made it famous in the grain markets of the world and insures for it the highest price. The berry is full and heavy, often exceeding by 5 to 9 pounds the standard weight of a bushel (60 pounds). There is practically no limit to the quantity which may be produced except in the lack of farmers to till the soil. The surplus yield in 1881 was enormous, considering the acreage. Not less than 300,000 tons, or 10,000,000 bushels, were offered for sale. Of this great quantity, Western Oregon and Washington produced 180,000 tons, and the country east of the Cascade Mountains yielded 120,000 tons. Up to November 15, 1881, there had been shipped to foreign ports, including vessels loading, 105,000 tons ; sent coast-wise, 15,000 tons ; probable future shipments to San Francisco, 35,000 tons ; total shipped or provided for, 155,000 tons ; amount remaining to be shipped, 145,000 tons ; tonnage on way to Portland, 80,000 tons ; leaving unprovided for, at tide-water, 65,000 tons. The inland means of transportation which existed in 1881 were also strained to their utmost capacity in moving so large a crop. But, before the harvest of 1882 is garnered, the facilities for moving grain to tide-water will be greatly increased. In another place it is shown to what extent the railroads are building main lines and opening branch lines in order to meet the growing demands upon them.

Oats also yield heavily and are exported largely from many points. The standard weight of a bushel of oats is 36 pounds, but the weight of 40 and 45 pounds to the bushel is not infrequent. Rye and barley are likewise profitably raised. In the more southern parts of Oregon corn also flourishes, but the average summer is too cool for this cereal in the northern sections of the country.

Hops are a very important product. They are grown on the river bottom lands, and, with proper cultivation, a large yield of superior quality is obtained. The crop runs from 1,500 to 3,000 pounds per acre. The principal gardens at present are in the Willamette Valley, Oregon, and in the Puyallup Valley, Washington Territory. The hop acreage might be profitably increased tenfold, as the crop sells readily at prices ranging from 15 to 20 cents per pound, and the export demand is steady. Some of the advantages connected with this industry are, the certainty of a good crop, the early bearing of the vines, the extraordinary yield, the low cost of production, the facilities for securing suitable soil, poles, fuel for drying and cheap (Indian) labor for picking. This crop has never suffered from insects or disease.

Of recent years flax has been raised for export, and its culture is a permanent industry. To produce it successfully requires particular care, but farmers find it an excellent crop to rotate with wheat, and the larger profits repay for the greater labor attending its cultivation. It is not unusual to obtain from 400 to 800 pounds of clean fibre per acre. The farmers in the neighborhood of Moscow, near the Idaho line, produced, in 1881, not less than 100,000 bushels of flax-seed, which netted them the same number of dollars. There is no doubt that linen making could be successfully engaged in, provided the necessary capital and labor could be secured for the enterprise, particularly as there is convenient water-power everywhere for driving any number of looms and mills.

Vegetables of every variety and of the finest quality are produced. Potatoes, cabbages, onions, turnips, squashes, beets, carrots, parsnips, cucumbers and celery grow to large size. The potato bug has never appeared and potato diseases are unknown. Onions produce immensely on the low-lying lands. All the vegetables named thrive equally well and give abundant crops in both sections of the country, notwithstanding the great climatic distinctions which exist east and west of the Cascade Mountains. Melons, tomatoes and some of the fruits, however, flourish better in the warmer and dryer atmosphere east of the mountains.

Fruits of delicious aroma and flavor and of remarkable size and beauty are abundant. Their culture must eventually prove a source of great profit, as the market for preserved and dried fruits is world-wide.

Apples grow to perfection. The tree is indigenous to the soil. The fruit of the orchards is large, highly colored, and of delicate taste. Trees are stout and hardy and so prolific that, without due care, they are likely to exhaust themselves by overbearing.

Prunes thrive as well as in any other part of the world. The trees are healthy and vigorous and bear quite early. They have hitherto been exempt from the ravages of the curculio. The fruit is rich, mellow, large and beautiful, and has a delicate aromatic taste. It is excellent for table use, and superior for drying and preserving.

Plums are prolific, sweet, and of fine flavor. There are many varieties and the trees are hardy and reliable bearers. Some kinds are magnificent in size and color.

Pears of all the best known varieties, early and late, are produced in profusion. The trees are hardy, bearing at a remarkably early age, and yielding sweet, mellow fruit which cannot be exceeded either in size or in flavor. Nothing is more delicious than the pears. Some specimens attain a weight of three pounds and upward.

Cherries, which cannot be excelled anywhere, grow in unlimited abundance. The trees are hardy and heavy bearers, and the fruit is so superior in size and beauty that its value for shipping and market purposes leaves nothing to be desired.

Peaches have been cultivated satisfactorily along the Columbia River and in the Walla Walla Valley, as well as at many other points east of the Cascade Mountains. With proper care the peach orchards may be made to yield not alone for home consumption but also for export.

Apricots, quinces and grapes may be profitably grown, and, indeed, they are produced to a greater or less extent. Many parts of the country are perfectly adapted to grapes, and even in those portions where the climate is naturally unsuitable to the vine on an extensive scale, there are always locations where grapes may be produced in limited quantities.

Strawberries, raspberries, blackberries, gooseberries and currants, delicious in flavor, large in size, and perfect in all respects, are easily raised and are quite abundant. Strawberries are often ripe by the first of May, and the other fruits follow in succession. The season for each kind of berry is more than ordinarily long, and the wild varieties of these fruits supplement those that are cultivated.

The preparation of all these fruits for market ought to be a leading industry. Intelligent enterprise in this direction is, indeed, much needed. The business of fruit raising would afford agreeable and lucrative occupation to many people who are unfitted for the more arduous work of ordinary farming, and the preparation of such products for market is an industry which would naturally become important. Attention to the capabilities of the country in this respect has been attracted to some extent, and numerous large orchards have been planted. The fruit-drying establishments which already exist at various places in Western Oregon find a ready market for their productions in New York, China, Japan, South America, Australia and elsewhere. Both fresh and dried apples, as well as plums and prunes, are shipped to San Francisco. But the business of drying and preserving fruits might be expanded indefinitely.

Grasses, both native and exotic, grow luxuriantly and in great variety. East of the Cascades there are at a low estimate 40,000,000 of acres of natural pasture lands, most of which produce the nutritious bunch grass. West of this range of mountains the variety of native grasses is very large. These grasses retain their fattening qualities until late in the autumn. Wild pea vine, which affords an excellent pasturage for stock, grows in great abundance on the foot-hills, especially where the timber has been destroyed by fire. Of the cultivated grasses, timothy is the staple kind for hay. Red and white clover yield heavily under proper cultivation, and alfalfa, blue, red-top and orchard grasses do well everywhere.

The relative productiveness of the soil, of course, varies according to its nature and the skill expended upon its cultivation. In the wheat-growing regions, with ordinary care in ploughing and sowing, the yield per acre, without manuring, will be from 20 to 35 bushels. With a higher cultivation, and still without the use of manure, the yield often exceeds this quantity, a fact apparent from the following letter, written by Dr. Blalock, under date of October 20, 1881. This gentleman's enormous wheat farm is situated in the very heart of a "sage bush tract," and to him is due the great honor of having discovered the vast agricultural capabilities of lands so uninviting. He wrote :

WALLA WALLA, October, 1881.

Inclosed please find statement of number of acres cultivated by me this year in this valley to wheat, and the average yield per acre of the same :

2,300 acres in one body, average .... 35¼   bushels per acre.
1,000 acres of same field,   "   50   "   "
459   "   "   "   "   .... 38$\frac{78}{100}$ "   "

The land was accurately surveyed by the county surveyor. The 1,000 acres was selected out of the best part of the field, then to this thousand was added 459 acres of the next best.

The wheat was sowed in October and harvested in July, August and September. We cut and threshed and hauled to market same day. This farm is what is known as foot-hill bunch-grass land, of which there is yet large areas of Government lands unoccupied and open for settlement.

Very respectfully,

N. G. BLALOCK

The average yield of wheat per acre may safely be stated at 22 bushels; of oats and barley, 35; of corn, in localities where it may be profitably raised, 40; of rye, 20; of peas, 40; of beans, 36; of potatoes, 300; of sweet potatoes, 150; of turnips, 600; of carrots, 500; of parsnips, 500. Cabbages produce from 1,500 to 2,000 pounds, and hay from two and a half to three tons per acre.

The ordinary harvest time for wheat is from June 24 to September 10; for oats, from July 13 to 20; for barley, from June 20 to July 1; for rye, from July 1 to 10; for corn, from August 20 to September 10.

Barns and sheds for keeping the grain, which are indispensable in other countries, are scarcely needed here. The grain is threshed in the fields by machinery, and thence sent in sacks directly to warehouses for storage or exportation. Neither mildew nor rust has appeared to any great extent, and no failure of the wheat crop has been known since the settlement of the country, thirty-seven years ago. Owing to the dry summers, the wheat is not affected by the long sea voyage to Great Britain, whither most of it is exported, and by the double passage through the tropics, incidental to its transportation.

TIMBER.

It would scarcely be possible to exaggerate the extent and value of the forests of this region. East and west of the Cascade Mountains there are large tracts of timber lands which the lumberman has not yet invaded. Many such tracts will be brought within the reach of markets on the completion of the transportation lines now in course of construction. In the Blue Mountains and on the eastern slopes of the Cascades the supply of timber is more than sufficient to cover the local demand. It will yield a large surplus for shipment to the level, timberless territories lying eastward. But west of the Cascade Mountains, and especially in Washington Territory, the lumberman must look for the material which will keep his mills at work without fear of exhausting the supply. The finest body of timber in the world is embraced between the Columbia River and British Columbia and the Pacific Ocean and the Cascades. At a very low estimate, one-half the growth of this Puget Sound district consists of trees which will yield 25,000 feet of lumber to the acre. The approximate quantity, therefore, in this great tract alone, the area of which is nearly as large as the State of Iowa, is not less than 160,000,000,000 feet. During the last thirty-five years the aggregate cut has been, perhaps, not more than 2,500,000,000 feet, leaving a supply of 157,500,000,000 feet from which to draw. The principal growths are fir, pine, spruce, cedar, larch and hemlock, although white oak, maple, cottonwood, ash, alder and other varieties are found in considerable quantities. Three kinds of cedar, two of fir, and three of pine are indigenous to the country. The fir, however, exceeds in quantity and value all the other species combined, and the cedar ranks second in this respect. Trees attain an unusual development, both with regard to height and to symmetry of form. Perhaps nowhere else are they found so tall, straight and gently-tapering as to fit them peculiarly for ships' spars and masts. The yellow fir is not infrequently 250 feet in height; the pine 120 to 160 feet; the silver fir, 150 feet; white cedar, 100 feet; white oak, 70 feet, and black spruce, 150 feet. Cedars have been found of 63 feet girth and 120 feet in height. The sugar pine of Oregon is equal to the best cedar. Ordinary sized trees yield 6,000 to 8,000 feet of lumber each, and many as much as 15,000. Of this are made railroad ties, boards, deals, fencing, laths, paling, pickets, barrel staves and heads, household furniture and ship-timber. The product of the saw-mills is shipped to San Francisco, the Sandwich Islands, Mexico, the Pacific Coast of South America, Australia and even to England and France, China and Japan. The first saw-mill was built on Puget Sound in 1851, with a capacity of 1,000 feet daily. In 1853, a steam saw-mill was erected at Seattle which could cut 8,000 to 10,000 feet per day. The business has since greatly increased. The largest saw-mill of the fifteen in operation on Puget Sound is that at Port Ludlow, with a cutting capacity of 200,000 feet per day. The other mills are situated at Port Gamble, Port Madison, Port Blakely, Port Discovery, Seabeck, Utsalada, Tacoma and New Tacoma, and the remainder at Seattle. The aggregate daily cutting capacity of these mills is over 1,000,000 feet. Some of the logs sawed are enormous in girth and sometimes 115 feet in length. Planing mills are attached to most of these large saw-mills, and dressed building lumber is obtained as required. Each mill is admirably situated with a view to economical production, and nearly every one of them comprises a town of itself, with stores, shops, steam-tugs, lumber-vessels and dwellings owned by the companies. Ship-building is also an important feature.

The export of lumber from Puget Sound during 1881 amounted to 174,176,700 feet, valued at $1,718,226. Of this, 41,760,700 feet, valued at $394,066, were shipped to foreign ports and the remainder coastwise. Owing to competition and to greater facilities of production, the price of lumber has steadily fallen in recent years in spite of the fact that the demand has constantly increased. The average price, in 1881, was $9.50 per thousand feet.

The existing conditions of lumbering at Puget Sound could not be more favorable. The forests remain for the most part in virgin condition, except for a short distance from the banks of the streams and estuaries; the shores are not so abrupt as to prevent easy handling of the timber; the harbors are numerous, deep and well sheltered; the hardships, losses and delays incident to severe winters are unknown; logs may be floated down the rivers without danger of a sudden rise and the breaking of "booms;" by clearing the river channels of drift, both logs and lumber may be run out for long distances, and rafts may be towed with ease on the waters of the Sound with only the ebb and flow of the tide to consider in moving them to points of shipment. In this way loggers bring logs from all the bodies of timber along the shore lines to the mills, and dispose of them at fair rates to the owners. This gives employment to hundreds of working men. There are still very many desirable places for establishing not only saw-mills, but factories for the manufacture of barrels, pails, house trimmings, doors, sashes, blinds, moulding and every other article made of wood. These opportunities are not confined to Puget Sound. They exist along the harbors and bays of the entire coast of Washington Territory and Oregon, and are only used as yet to a comparatively small extent. For some purposes, and particularly in the manufacture of beautiful household furniture, the ornamental woods of Oregon are unsurpassed.

SAW-MILL ON PUGET SOUND, W. T.

FISHERIES.

The waters of Oregon and Washington Territory abound in fish, of which many varieties are of great commercial value. Particularly is this the fact with regard to salmon. Every river on the coast line teems with this fish, of which there are several species, all excellent in flavor, and many being noted for immense size and weight. These salmon are easily taken, and, being well adapted for canning and salting, a great and prosperous business in connection with them is carried on at several places. Especially is this the case on the Columbia River where the business of salmon packing is one of the principal industries. The good quality of the Columbia River fish has given it a far-famed reputation, and the demand for it is unlimited. In addition to the large market for this commodity in the Eastern States, it is sold extensively in Australia, England and other European countries. This business is likely to be permanent, and it is capable of indefinite expansion, constantly adding to the enrichment of the country. This industry was established on the Columbia River in the year 1866, the sales of the first year amounting to the encouraging sum of $64,000. The progress which has since been made and the importance which the business has reached within a period of sixteen years, is seen at a glance by the following statistics :

Year.	Product.	Case Price.	Total Value.
1866	4,000	$16 00	$64,000
1867	18,000	13 00	234,000
1868	28,000	12 00	336,000
1869	100,000	10 00	1,000,000
1870	150,000	9 00	1,350,000
1871	200,000	9 50	1,900,000
1872	250,000	8 00	2,000,000
1873	250,000	7 00	1,750,000
1874	350,000	6 50	2,275,000
1875	375,000	5 60	2,100,000
1876	450,000	4 50	2,025,000
1877	460,000	5 20	2,392,000
1878	460,000	5 00	2,300,000
1879	480,000	4 60	2,188,000
1880	550,000	4 80	2,640,000
1881	530,000	5 00	2,650,000

Thirty-five canneries on the Columbia River, between the Cascades and the town of Astoria, near the entrance of the stream, share in this enterprise. Cans of ordinary size hold one pound each, and there are forty-eight cans in each case. Estimating the weight of the case, including the cans, at 72 pounds, the pack of 1881 was about 19,000 tons, and toward the close of the season the catch was so enormous that many fish were thrown away for lack of canning facilities. Although competition has reduced the wholesale price of a case of salmon from $16, in 1866, to $5, in 1881, and the sum paid the fishermen for each fish has increased during that interval of time from ten cents to sixty-five, the profit of the canning establishments continue to be satisfactory. In this business on the Columbia, a capital of at least $2,000,000 is invested, and all the operations must be conducted with the utmost system and economy to insure success. The fish are taken with gill nets, seines and traps. In 1881, the number of boats employed was 1,650, including ten steam tenders. The cost of a boat fully equipped with net is about $600. The gill nets used are from 250 to 300 fathoms long and 20 feet deep. The seines are from 100 to 200 yards long. The boats and nets are generally owned by the proprietors of the canneries, who lease them with the necessary implements and supplies to the fishermen on the condition that one-third of the catch is to be paid for rent and the remaining two-thirds must be sold to the owner at a stipulated price. Each boat will catch on an average 2,000 fish during the season. With the exception of a few Indians, the fishermen are white men, chiefly Scandinavians and Italians. About 7,500 men are employed during the season. Of these, however, over 3,500 are Chinese laborers, engaged in the canneries doing the lighter work.

Three average salmon will fill four dozen cans. The fishing is at its height for three months, from May to July, but the most abundant run in later years has been toward the last weeks of the season. Artificial hatching has been resorted to in order to maintain the supply, and with judicious legislation to protect the fish there is no reason to fear their eventual extirpation.

Beside the salmon fisheries on the Columbia River, similar establishments, many of great importance, exist on the Willamette, the Umpqua and Rogue rivers, and, particularly, on the waters of Puget Sound. The fish, differing much in quality and value, abound literally in millions. They crowd the seas, bays, estuaries and the smaller rivers which flow into the ocean at certain seasons of the year, and may be easily caught with gill nets and with the hook. There is ample opportunity still for the healthy growth of the salmon fishing industry in the North-west region.

In addition to salmon, the streams of Oregon and Washington Territory abound in various kinds of delicious trout. Sturgeon of immense size are found at the mouths of all the larger rivers. The lakes and ponds teem with fish of several species, among which may be mentioned the lake-trout, the perch and the pike. Oysters and clams are taken in the bays. Halibut of enormous size, and of a delicacy and tenderness not known in its Atlantic congener, makes its habitat in the waters of Puget Sound. The eulachon, a delicious fish, about the size of a small herring, is found in enormous quantities all along the coast. Codfish, averaging two and one-half feet in length, and with a girth around the shoulders of eighteen inches, are taken in the Sound, but they fairly shoal the waters of the banks on which they live, beginning at the western extremity of Vancouver Island and extending beyond Alaska. Herrings and smelts are plentiful. Whales and seals are also found along the coast. These and other denizens of the waters abound in inexhaustible supply, needing only capital and labor to establish fisheries in this part of the country which would prove as productive and as profitable as any on the face of the globe.

MINERALS.

The mineral wealth of Oregon and Washington Territory is large and diversified. Not only are the precious metals obtained, but coal, iron, and other useful minerals exist in lavish quantities at many points throughout the country. The production of gold has been going on constantly during the last thirty years, and the coal and iron interests have also, of late, assumed considerable importance. But, as a rule, the mining industries are yet in their infancy.

Gold was discovered in Jackson and Josephine Counties, Southern Oregon, in 1851. Some time afterwards auriferous gravel was found in large quantities in Baker and Grant Counties, Eastern Oregon. At various times, also, placer and quartz mining have been carried on, respectively, at Coos Bay and in the extreme southern part of the Cascade Mountains, in Oregon. In Washington Territory, likewise, the Colville country, and the bed of the Skagit River, have yielded more or less of the precious metal. Perhaps the entire quantity obtained during the past thirty years has not been less than $40,000,000, more than half of which is to be credited to the first decade in which gold mining was prosecuted. Hitherto, as a rule, operations, in all their phases, have been conducted in a very superficial manner. True, some wonderfully rich deposits have been found, and worked with great profit. But only arastras and other primitive methods for crushing the quartz have been used. Claims were generally abandoned after the surface gravel was exhausted. The expense and labor of sinking shafts, driving tunnels, and employing the other scientific and profitable methods now in vogue, have not been applied. There seems at present, however, to be a disposition to prosecute gold mining with ordinary skill and vigor. Companies have been formed with the capital necessary to develop the real value of the deposits. Several claims have been opened at various points, on which large amounts have been expended for the requisite machinery to carry on hydraulic mining on a large scale.

Coal will take a foremost rank among the mineral resources which are hereafter to be a prime factor in the growth and development of the country. The abundant supply of this raw material will keep in motion many prosperous industries. Immense beds of semi-bituminous and lignite coal are known to underlie many parts of the region. Especially is this the fact west of the Cascade Mountains. This mineral exists in Oregon, at Coos Bay, in Coos County, on the northern Umpqua, and in other localities in Douglas County. It is found at Yaquina Bay, at Port Oxford, near St. Helens, on Pass Creek, on the line of the Oregon and California Railroad, and at different points in Clackamas, Clatsop and Tillamook Counties. At most of these places the beds have only been partially explored. The Coos Bay mines are quite valuable, one of them being capable of an output of 1,000 tons a day, if necessary, and they represent an invested capital of $2,000,000. The principal market for the Coos Bay coal is at San Francisco, whither it is conveyed by small sailing vessels and two small steam colliers. The coal fields of Washington Territory, at Puget Sound, however, are far more extensive than those of Oregon. At a very early day in the history of the Territory indications of coal were discovered. In 1863 deposits were found on Issaqua Creek, near Samamish Lake, and on Coal Creek, near Lake Washington. A very important coal mine is at Newcastle, near Seattle. It is owned by the Oregon Improvement Company, and its product is a pure lignite, well adapted to household and railway purposes. The coal fields are connected by a narrow-gauge railroad with Seattle, the shipping port, 22 miles distant. The company have a fleet of four new steam colliers, each vessel averaging two and one-half trips a month between Seattle and San Francisco. These steamers were built at Chester, Pa., expressly for this trade. The coal beds at Newcastle are practically inexhaustible, and the yield becomes cleaner and harder the deeper the veins are worked. The output from this mine alone, known as the Seattle, in 1881, was not short of 150,000 tons, and the quantity mined this year will be considerably greater, in consequence of increased transportation facilities. The total output during the ten years since this mine has been in operation has been 800,000 tons. Other coal fields on Puget Sound exist on Carbon, Cedar and Green rivers, specimens from which indicate an excellent quality. The Puyallup River coal deposits are also very valuable. Here thirty distinct veins have been found, in three different groups, varying from three feet up to nine, fourteen and even eighteen feet thick. To the Puyallup coal region a branch line of the Northern Pacific Railroad was built in 1876, terminating at Wilkeson, 31 miles from New Tacoma. Excellent coal is also obtained at Carbonado, on the Carbon River, and at numerous other points in the Territory. The mines at present worked are the Seattle, Renton, Seaton, Wilkeson and Carbonado.

Iron ore, bog, hematite, and magnetic, exist in great masses, and may be easily obtained. It abounds on the Columbia River, extending from a point opposite Kalama, southward, almost to the falls of the Willamette River. It is also found in large deposits in the Counties of Columbia, Tillamook, Marion, Clackamas, Jackson and Coos. Smelting furnaces are already established at Oswego, on the Willamette River, eight miles south of Portland, and near Port Townsend, in Washington Territory, at which latter place a rich bog ore is obtained. The pig iron produced at these furnaces is of excellent quality, and is largely used at the local foundries. Iron ore has been, likewise, recently found on the western slopes of the Cascade Mountains. With this abundance of iron and coal there is ample opportunity for developing important manufacturing interests.

There are likewise deposits at various points, of copper, lead, tin, zinc, cinnabar, plumbago, gypsum, kaolin, pottery clays, mica, marble, granite, limestone and sandstone. All these, in time, will assuredly attract the attention which they deserve, and be made to yield handsome returns.

LIVE STOCK.

Oregon and Washington Territory are undoubtedly the best country for cattle in the United States, not even excepting Texas, is the opinion of stock-raisers. The general practice of farmers west of the Cascade Mountains is to provide fodder for only a part of the year, and to allow their cattle to roam at large the remainder of the time. In the cold weather stock suffers sometimes; but, as a rule, it does well enough in the open air throughout the year, subsisting on the abundant natural pasturage. The region most favorable to herding on a large scale is in the vast tracts of open country in Eastern Oregon and Washington. Here, immense droves are raised, and from one hundred and fifty thousand to two hundred thousand head of cattle are driven East every year over the mountains and across the plains to market. As a general thing, the animals get through the winter without other feed than that supplied by grazing on wild grass. The extreme cold weather is never so cold, even for a day at a time, as the extreme cold weather of Illinois and New York. The largest owners of horned stock are doing much to improve its quality by infusing short-horn blood into the herds. In the Willamette Valley there are several breeders of Short-Horns, Holsteins, Jerseys, Alderneys and Devons of pure race, the latter being well adapted to the peculiarities of country and climate.

Horses of an excellent type are largely raised. The soil and climate, combined with good blood, have succeeded in producing not only the best kind of draught animals, but also good trotters, roadsters and carriage horses. Great attention is given to this matter, and much money has been invested in obtaining fine imported stock, from the heaviest Percherons and Clydesdales to the fleetest thoroughbreds. The horses raised east of the Cascade Mountains excel those produced elsewhere in speed. This is due to the vast ranges of open, hilly country, the abundance of bunch-grass pasturage and the distance to the water-ing-places. Sometimes the animals go for ten miles on a fast trot from their feeding-places to water, thereby developing muscle from the time of their birth. In the bunch-grass districts great numbers of horses are economically raised, the feed costing nothing.

Sheep-husbandry is one of the greatest and most productive industries. The business is carried on throughout the entire region, under the most favorable con-ditions of climate that can anywhere be found. Eligible locations for pursuing this branch of enterprise in a country so large are to be found without limit. In Middle and South-eastern Oregon, as well as in Eastern Washington Territory, there are thousands upon thousands of acres which are eminently fitted for pasturing sheep, and which are not occupied to within twenty per cent. of their capacity. The number of the flocks increases year by year, however, sheep not being so much affected by railroads and wheat fields as cattle, and the indications are that sheep-husbandry will grow to still greater proportions for a long time to come. There is no doubt that this business, conducted on intelligent principles, is certain to yield large profits. This has been repeatedly proved by experience. The wool produced has obtained a reputation of its own in the markets of New York and Boston, and is fast taking rank with the best fleeces which reach the East. The fibre is uniform, showing no weak spots in all its length, thereby attesting the fact of its growth in a climate to which extremes of heat and cold are unknown. The industry of wool-growing has been of sufficiently long standing to admit of improving the breed. This has been done by enterprising growers, and rams of the best merino and long-wool blood have been imported for the purpose. That wool has become a staple of commerce is shown by the fact that in 1881 the clip was over 8,000,000 pounds.

With regard to the bunch-grass pasturage for live stock of all kinds east of the mountains, it may be said, that it affords all the elements of nutriment neces-sary for bone, muscle and flesh. It is quite as strong as oats or barley, and the quantity of this grass which an animal will eat in a day will supply it with as much nourishment as the quantity of timothy, clover or hay it will eat in the same time, with the usual amount of grain added. It is found, in the work of grading the Northern Pacific Railroad, that the horses and mules which graze upon bunch-grass during the winter have a better appearance, and do better work than those fed upon hay and grain. At noon a ration of oats must be given to working animals, simply because this is a condensed form of food, and the time allowed for feeding at that hour is not sufficient for them to get the needed quantity of grass. At one time the contractor was breaking to work forty young colts which had never tasted grain, but ran wild each winter on the bunch-grass upon which they had matured. They looked like grain-fed animals, and a remarkable feature was, that while they were well rounded, hard and solid in flesh, they were not large bellied like animals fed on ordinary grass. The farmers and stock-men, therefore, do not use grain, because the animals keep in excellent condition without it. Horses employed on the railroad grade are turned out at night, and before morning they get enough food to work on. This bunch-grass matures early in summer, and stands the year through, curing in the warm months without loss of strength. It grows in well-defined tussocks, several inches apart, and to all heights under thirty inches, the spears being round and fine like wire, and quite strong and tough. In some places on the hill tops and upper lands the grass is so heavy that a ton could be cut to the acre, and if cut and fed to stock they want nothing more. Besides this bunch grass, there is another wild variety of value for hay which is called rye grass. This grows to a much greater height than bunch-grass, and has broad flat leaves, some of which are over an inch in width.

ZOOLOGY.

There are many wild animals common to the country, and opportunities for hunting and shooting cannot be surpassed. Black bears are numerous, and east of the Cascade Mountains the grizzly bear is sometimes captured. Of the deer family, elk of large size are in great abundance, as well as the black-tail, the Virginia, and, on the Spokane Plains, the mule deer. The cougar or panther, and many of the smaller felidæ, are to be found. There are several varieties of foxes and wolves. The beaver, the badger, seals, both hair and fur ; the raccoon, the marten, the mink, the fish and land otter, the musk-rat, the weasel, the skunk, and several kinds of rabbits and squirrels are plentiful. Among the birds of passage are many varieties of swans, geese and ducks. There are also other aquatic fowl. The grouse family is well represented, and quail and snipe of large size are numerous. Song birds and birds of prey, in very great variety of species, are common.

EDUCATION AND RELIGION.

Both Oregon and Washington Territory are alive to the importance of education and public morals, and, relatively to the population, schools and churches are quite liberally supported.

The school fund of Oregon is in part provided from the proceeds of sales of land which was granted to the State by Congress for educational purposes, but the larger part of the income is derived from a direct tax of from three to four mills, which is imposed by the Legislature. Recent statistics showed that the pupils enrolled in the public schools numbered 37,533, and the average daily attendance was 27,435. There were 1,007 school districts and 934 school-houses. Forty-five of these schools were for scholars of advanced grade. The average time school was maintained in each district was four months and a half. The total number of teachers was 1,314, of whom 635 were male and 679 female. The average monthly pay of the men was $44.19, and of the women, $33.38. Total expenditures for the year were $307,031, and the value of the school property was $567,863. There were also 142 private schools, with an attendance of 4,200, among which 15 were classed as academies and 12 as collegiate schools. The latter were founded and are conducted under the auspices of the Episcopal, Presbyterian, Baptist, Roman Catholic and other churches. Teachers' Institutes hold annual meetings in each judicial district. For higher educational purposes there are four (so-called) universities, which are in reality only collegiate institutions. These are: the State University, at Eugene City; the Willamette University, at Salem, a Methodist college, with a medical department connected with it; the Pacific University and Tualatin Academy, at Forest Grove, which is non-sectarian in character, and the Blue Mountain University, at La Grande, Eastern Oregon. There are also four colleges, one of which is the Corvallis College, situated at the town of the same name, under the management of the Methodist Episcopal Church South. To this institution is attached the State Agricultural College, endowed by Congress with a grant of 90,000 acres of the public land, which is doing good service. The other colleges are respectively known as McMinnville College, at McMinnville, which is under the control of the Baptists; Philomath College, at Philomath, directed by the United Brethren in Christ (Moravian), and Christian College, at Monmouth, with which is connected a normal school. These institutions are generally well attended in all the classes, and each of them admits women to the several departments. There is also at Portland a college for women, St. Helen's Hall, under the care of the Protestant Episcopal Church. The State University is reported to be in a flourishing condition, and fairly meets the anticipations of its most ardent friends. It has a numerous corps of professors and tutors, and is well supplied with apparatus and collections. The grant of land made by Congress toward its foundation was 66,080 acres, of which about 20,000 acres remain unsold. The State also supports establishments for the education of the blind and for deaf mutes.

Educational matters in Washington Territory are very much on the same basis as they are in Oregon. There are in each township 1,280 acres set apart by the United States Government for school purposes, but these lands have not yet been sold so largely as to supply more than the nucleus of a school fund. That the foundation, however, for a generous support of the public schools has been made, is shown by the legislative appropriation of $100,000 from the Common School fund in 1880, which amount was apportioned among the several counties. The territorial revenue laws provide also for a tax of three to four mills for the support of the schools. Seattle, Walla Walla, and other of the larger towns have graded schools, and the aim is always toward thoroughness and efficiency. In 1879, there were 378 school districts, 326 school-houses, besides 14 temporary school-rooms. Of the 17,173 persons of school age, 11,540 children were enrolled. The number of teachers employed was 323, of whom 136 were men and 167 women, the general average of monthly pay being $45. The University of Washington Territory, situated at Seattle, is a part of the public school system, and has a normal department attached. It has an average of 150 students in its four departments. There are many well-conducted private academies in the Territory also, among which may be named the College of the Holy Angels at Vancouver, a Roman Catholic institution, with about 100 pupils.

From the latest available statistics (those of 1875) it appeared that there were in Oregon 351 religious organizations of all denominations, with 242 church edifices, 320 clergymen, 14,334 communicants, and 71,630 adherents. The assessed value of the church property was $654,000. With respect to numbers, these reli-

ASTORIA, OREGON, ENTRANCE TO COLUMBIA RIVER.

gious organizations rank as follows : Methodists, Baptists, Presbyterians, Roman Catholics, Episcopalians, Congregationalists, and five minor sects. Since the date named there has been a large increase of the population of the State, with a corresponding augmentation of the churches. It is estimated that in Washington Territory there are 135 church edifices, and the same number of pastors, with church property to the value of $150,000. All the denominations are represented, the Methodists here also leading in numbers, followed by the Roman Catholics, next the Baptists, and after these, in their order, the United Brethren, the Episcopalians, the Presbyterians, the Congregationalists, and the smaller sects.

CITIES AND TOWNS.

Portland is the commercial metropolis of the entire region. The city is situated on the Willamette River, twelve miles above its confluence with the Columbia. The population in 1870, including that of East Portland, was 11,103. This had swollen in 1880 to 23,000 souls, and the ratio of increase in future is certain to be very much higher. The reasons for this are quite obvious. Portland's growth and progress are based upon the solid foundation of natural advantages of position. Its site is so admirable that the limits of the city may be extended on every side. It is virtually a sea-port, to which large vessels may come direct from any part of the world and find wharf accommodation. It lies in the very heart of a great producing country which has no other outlet, and for which it must serve as a receiver and distributor of exports and imports. At no other point in the Pacific North-west are these manifest superiorities offered. In this connection it may be remarked that the navigation of the waters of the Willamette and the Columbia Rivers is only made difficult by obstructions that are caused by parsimony and neglect. The channels of these streams may be kept clear by a comparatively small annual outlay upon the bars and shoals. Portland is the seat of a steamship company which runs lines of ocean steamers to San Francisco and Puget Sound, British Columbia and Alaska, as well as a fleet of river boats. It is likewise the centre of a railway system which, within the year 1882, will have 2,000 miles of road in operation, and bring the city a heavy commercial tribute. Its streets are wide, regularly laid out, well paved and well lighted. The buildings of the business thoroughfares would do credit to any city, and the same may be said of many of the churches, the post-office, the custom-house, and other public edifices, as well as private residences. The markets are good and spacious. There are public and other schools of various grades, a large library, well-conducted newspapers, banks, commodious hotels, street cars, water, gas, manufacturing establishments, telegraphic communication with all parts of the world, an immense wholesale and retail business, and, in fine, all the features of a flourishing modern city. The permanent advancement of Portland is guaranteed by the air of substantial prosperity which pervades the place. The volume of business is greater than can be shown by any other city of its size in the United States. Interesting facts with reference to the shipping and export trade of Portland are given under the head of " Commerce," on another page.

PUBLIC SCHOOL BUILDINGS, PORTLAND, OREGON.

Other thriving towns and cities in Oregon, with their respective populations, as given by the United States census of 1880, are: Salem, the State capital, 52 miles south of Portland, on the Willamette River, and the county seat of Marion County, 2,538; Astoria, the county seat of Clatsop County, situated 12 miles from the mouth of the Columbia River, with fine advantages as a port of shipment, and for commerce generally, 2,803; Oregon City, county seat of Clackamas County, an important manufacturing town, with unlimited water-power, 1,263; Corvallis, in Benton County, seat of the State Agricultural College and present terminus of the West Side Division of the Oregon and California Railroad, 1,128; The Dalles, a flourishing city on the Columbia River, in Wasco County, 2,232; Roseburg, in Douglas County, leading town in the Umpqua Valley, and terminus of the Oregon and California Railroad, 822: Jacksonville, in Jackson County, the largest town in the Rogue River Valley, with an active business, 839: Baker City, a flourishing town in Baker County, in the midst of a mining and agricultural region, and also prominent as the terminus of two nearly completed railroad lines, 1,258; Albany, with its precinct, an important wheat centre in the Willamette Valley, 3,517; Eugene City, seat of the State University, also in the Willamette Valley, 1,170. Besides the places named are many more of much prominence which are particularly mentioned in the appendix in a description of the counties to which they belong.

In Washington Territory the principal towns are Olympia, the capital, with 1,232 inhabitants; Seattle, the most important point on Puget Sound, with a steadily growing commerce in coal, lumber, fish, etc., 3,533; New Tacoma, terminus of the Pacific Division of the Northern Pacific Railroad, also on Puget Sound, 1,098; Port Townsend, the port of entry for the Puget Sound Customs' District, 917; Vancouver, on the Columbia River, headquarters of the U. S. Army for the Department of the Columbia, 1,722; and, in Eastern Washington Territory, Walla Walla, a prosperous city, the centre of what is at present the most fertile wheat-producing region, connected by railroad with Portland, 3,588; Dayton, with a woolen manufactory, and also in railroad connection, doing a great business in wheat, 996; Colfax, 444; Spokane Falls, 350; Yakima City, 267; Palouse City, 148; the latter being agricultural towns.

THE WILLAMETTE VALLEY.

This valley, famed alike for its beauty, salubrity and fertility, is situated in Western Oregon. From north to south, its length is 125 miles, and its average breadth the entire distance is over forty. A better idea of its great size may be gained by remembering that its area is larger than that of Vermont or New Hampshire, Massachusetts or New Jersey, nearly as large as that of Maryland, almost three times as large as that of Connecticut, five times as large as that of Delaware and ten times larger than that of Rhode Island. On either hand it is hemmed in by wooded mountains, from the defiles of which numerous lateral valleys debouch upon it. The whole of its wide expanse is refreshed and beautified by more than forty water-courses which feed the navigable river of the same name that flows through it. The valley presents the most charming alternations of scenery, including every feature from snow-capped mountain peaks to thickly wooded hills, rich meadows, shady groves and pastoral dales. In view of its manifold attractions, it has been not inappropriately termed " the Eden of Oregon." Although the earliest settlers established their homes in this valley, and it is now, as it has been always, the most populous portion of the State, embracing within its limits the most important towns and cities, it still offers vast tracts of agricultural lands to cultivators. Within its natural boundaries—the Columbia River on the north, the Cascade Mountains on the east, the Coast Range on the west, and the Callapoia Mountains on the south—it contains four millions of acres, of which area nearly the whole is of unusual productiveness. But to assume that one-fifth of this land is now under cultivation, or even held in permanent meadows for pasturing and grazing purposes, would be estimating very liberally.

The staple productions of the Willamette Valley are all the cereals, with the exception of Indian corn, wool, cattle, fruit and vegetables. Wheat raising, however, for which the soil and climate are particularly adapted, takes the first rank in order of importance. Under favorable conditions of cultivation the yield is 20 to 30 bushels per acre, and even as much as 40 bushels. Land summer-fallowed and fall-sowed is certain to produce 25 bushels as a minimum yield. In some parts of this valley where the fields have been cropped continuously for a quarter of a century they still produce enormously, thus demonstrating the great strength and permanent qualities of the soil. The wheat of this region is a plump, full berry, from which flour of uncommon whiteness is made. Its excellence in this respect is so fully recognized that in the English markets it commands a premium of from three to five cents a bushel over the best produced in California. Many varieties of wheat are cultivated. The old white winter wheat, originally introduced by the Hudson Bay Company, is excellent in quality and retains its hold on popular favor. White velvet wheat is certainly as good, and perhaps more productive. Spring varieties of white wheat, Chili Club, Little Club, Australian and others, are well liked and give good crops. The peculiarities of the soil in the various counties mainly determine, however, the kind of wheat which is used for seed in different localities.

The principal owners of unoccupied lands in the valley are the United States Government and the Oregon and California and the Oregon Central Railroad companies. The lands owned by these corporations were obtained under a grant in aid of the construction of their railroads. These land grants, of course, were made long subsequent to the passage of the " Donation Law," the provisions of which have been elsewhere stated. Congress undoubtedly benefited the State by the law in question, in so far as a large immigration was thereby attracted. But what was originally an advantage has since proved a detriment. The lands taken up in large tracts by the pioneers were naturally those which could be cultivated with least labor. In this way the most easily tilled lands of Western Oregon and the rich prairies of the Willamette Valley fell into comparatively few hands. Unfortunately, the class who now hold these choice acres are, as a general thing, too unenergetic to cultivate all they possess, and at the same time too unwilling to dispose of what they do not use to those who would render the soil productive. Under these circumstances both the public and railroad lands of the Willamette Valley consist mainly of timber tracts, which are not so easily brought under cultivation. The lands in question for the most part are situated along the foot-hills

FIRST STREET, PORTLAND, OREGON.

of the Cascade and Coast ranges. Experience has amply proved that when the trees and undergrowth have once been cleared away, these timber-lands are quite as valuable for agricultural purposes as the best prairies. Over large areas destructive fires have already swept off the forests so effectively that the ground, at very little expense, may be entirely cleared for ploughing. Immense tracts of brush-lands in Benton, Yamhill, Marion, Polk and Clackamas counties, long supposed to be worthless, have recently been cleared and put under profitable cultivation. As illustrating how little was formerly known as to the value and productiveness of these brush-lands, the Waldo Hills region may be instanced. These hills are near Salem, contiguous to good highways, to railroads and steamboats. The soil is red and rich and easily worked. A few years ago the Waldo Hills were believed to be sterile and almost worthless. They are now the richest grain fields in the valley, producing the best samples of wheat that were shown at the Centennial and Paris Exhibitions of 1876 and 1878, and last year yielding 350,000 bushels. To-day the cleared portions sell readily from $30 to $50 an acre, exclusive of improvements.

The grants to the Oregon and California Railroad Company comprise the odd-numbered alternate sections within twenty miles of the road on either side, to the extent of 12,800 acres for every mile of road. This company sells its lands on the liberal terms of $1.25 to $7 per acre. If the purchaser pay cash he is allowed a discount of 10 per cent. on the price. If he choose to buy on credit he may take ten years to make up the amount in small annual payments, with interest at 7 per cent. per annum. Paying one-tenth of the purchase money at once, at the expiration of one year he pays 7 per cent. interest on the remaining nine tenths of the principal. At the close of the second year, he pays one-tenth of the principal and one year's interest on the remainder. In this way the payments go on each successive year, until all are made.

THE PALOUSE COUNTRY.

Perhaps settlers could find no more favorable region in which to establish themselves than in that part of Whitman County, W. T., which is known as the Palouse Country. This tract is situated between the Snake River on the south and the main line of the Northern Pacific Railroad on the north and west, and lies within the great grain-growing belt of the Columbia River Valley. Its merits for agricultural purposes have not been unrecognized, in view of the fact that railroad facilities have been supplied in order to forward its rapid settlement. The face of the country may fairly be described as high, rolling prairies. It is traversed by many streams, chief among which are the Palouse River and Rebel and Union Flat Creeks, with their numerous tributaries. Pure spring water almost everywhere abounds. In healthfulness the region is unsurpassed. The dryness of the climate secures comparative exemption from throat and lung troubles, rheumatism and fevers, and the invigorating air admits of great physical exertion with the minimum of discomfort

The soil of the Palouse Country is highly productive, and its constituents insure its lasting qualities. Its average depth is about three feet, except on the southern hill-slopes, where a slight admixture of clay is sometimes detected. It is, as a rule, equally productive on any spot where the plow can be used.

Wheat is the leading agricultural product of the Palouse Country. A heavy yield, varying from thirty-five to fifty bushels per acre, is usual. The quality of the crop leaves nothing to be desired. But bounteous harvests are not character-istic of wheat alone. Oats, barley, rye, timothy, flax, millet, potatoes, cabbage, beets, and, in fine, all the hardy cereals and vegetables, produce largely.

The unsettled lands of all this region, hill and valley alike, are covered with wild flowers and bunch-grass, which are a sure indication of the fertility of the ground. The abundance of this growth, and the nutritive properties of the grass, made this particular region a favorite pasture-range for cattle-raisers during many years. Of late, however, the ranchmen have been driven farther afield, because the fertility of the country has rendered it more valuable for agricultural pur-poses. The bunch-grass grows luxuriantly until about the middle of July, at which period it begins to be turned by the sun into excellent hay. Upon this wild grass stock subsist all the year round; although, particularly as far as horned cattle are concerned, it is always a risk to be unprepared with hay for winter feed-ing. The breeding of all kinds of stock is a prosperous occupation. Especially is this true of horses and sheep. Unlike horned cattle, these animals rarely need to be foddered, or even sheltered, at any time. They thrive finely upon the bunch-grass, pawing the snow away to get at it during the winter. The fecundity of the domestic animals is surprising, and this insures large profits.

The Palouse Country is not only within the limits of the land-grant of the Northern Pacific Railroad, by which line it is traversed, but it is also brought into connection with the principal centres of business and population in the entire Pacific North-west region by the Oregon Railway and Navigation Company's lines.

THE GRANDE RONDE VALLEY.

This remarkably beautiful and fertile valley is situated in Union County, Eastern Oregon, east of the Blue Mountains. It is about 25 miles long by 20 wide, and contains about 250,000 acres of excellent farming land. The soil is well adapted to the production of wheat, oats, barley, rye, flax, hemp, sugar beets and every sort of vegetables. The country can not be excelled for the purpose of dairying and stock-raising. The Grande Ronde Valley is almost surrounded by high mountains, the summits of which are covered with snow from early in November until late in July. The scenery is extremely beautiful, the eye never wearying of the grandeur of the mountains and the charms of the peaceful valley. Along the base of the mountains and within easy access of almost any part of the valley are fine bodies of timber consisting principally of pine, fir and tamarack. There are numerous streams of water threading the valley, which afford ample power for driving mills and machinery, and serve as well for irrigating in times of drought, although for the latter purpose there has been thus far very rarely occasions to use them. The climate of the Grande Ronde Valley is delightful and remarkably healthy, the air being pure and bracing. Pulmonary complaints have never been known to originate there, and cases of this disease which were considered hopeless have been cured by a residence in the valley. The altitude of the Grande Ronde is 3,000 feet above the level of the sea. Its coldest record was 18° below zero and its hottest about 96°. Owing to its isolation the valley has been comparatively overlooked by immigrants who have moved up the Columbia River. Its settlers have been chiefly persons who had crossed the plains in search of homes and were arrested by the favorable opportunities which this region offered.

There are four flourishing towns in Grande Ronde Valley. They are Union, the county-seat, with a population of over 800; La Grande, with about the same number, and Island City and Summerville, each having three hundred inhabitants. The mining camps in Union and Baker counties, and over the border in Idaho, have always afforded a fair market for the large quantities of flour and bacon produced in the valley, while droves of horses and herds of cattle are driven every year to Montana and Wyoming and there sold at a good profit. Grande Ronde Valley is distant from the Columbia 100 miles, and from Portland 220 miles. Excellent opportunities are offered for the purchase of both wild lands and improved farms. A large part of the land in the valley was selected by the State to fill a grant made by Congress for internal improvements. As these lands could only be purchased from the State in small parcels, never exceeding 320 acres to a single person, consequently they have not fallen into the hands of speculators. The price per acre of the State lands is fixed at $1.25. More desirable lands, well situated without improvements, can be bought at from $4 to $8 per acre.

LA CONNER, ARCHIPELAGO DE HARO, ETC.

An interesting and very fertile part of Washington Territory is that which is locally known as the La Conner Region, situated in Whatcom County, and also the contiguous mainland, as well as the adjacent islands in the Gulf of Georgia.

The village of La Conner is situated on rising ground, at the outlet of the north pass of the Skagit River, about 40 miles from the United States boundary line and 55 miles from Seattle, and has a population of 200, with 550 inhabitants in the precinct.

The Skagit is the largest river emptying into Puget Sound, and is navigable to its rapids, a distance of 80 miles from its mouth. Some of the finest timber on the Sound is on the upper reaches of the Skagit river, and towards the mouth of this stream it is estimated that there are about 50,000 acres of good farming lands, including the so-called tide-lands. These tide-lands are reclaimed temporarily by diking, at a cost of $30 per acre; but durable work requires an expenditure of perhaps double that amount.

Opposite the village of La Conner, on Fidalgo Island, there is an Indian reservation. These Indians, numbering about 200, have about six sections of land, or over 4,200 acres, mainly timber lands. They do little farming, although they have reclaimed some of the marshes.

On the Skagit River, and on the tide-lands which form its delta, there are about 20,000 acres under cultivation, of which 12,000 acres are tide-lands. The soil of the tide-lands is extremely rich, being composed of the alluvium deposited by the river. Mr. Conner, the largest proprietor, plants annually 600 acres in oats, barley and wheat—principally oats. The yield from oats is from 75 to 110 bushels per acre, or from $1\frac{1}{4}$ to 2 tons. The standard weight of a bushel of oats is 36 pounds, but the La Conner oats often weigh 45 pounds per bushel, and the average is probably 40 pounds. The farmers of the La Conner precinct had seven steam-threshers at work in 1881, each machine costing about $2,000. It is estimated that these engines threshed during the season 6,840 tons, or over 342,000 bushels of grain—mainly oats. For oats they received $22 a ton from produce dealers on the field, without hauling or any other labor beside threshing and sack-filling. This price was nearly $1\frac{1}{8}$ cents per pound, or 40 cents per bushel. In addition to oats the La Conner region produces barley and wheat, for which, respectively, $23 and $25 per ton were paid on the farms. The yield of timothy hay and clover is said to be from $2\frac{1}{2}$ to 3 tons per acre, and this sells readily in British Columbia at $10 per ton. Potatoes grow well on the uplands, and from 300 to 500 bushels per acre is a common crop. Apples attain large size and are of excellent flavor. All the hardier vegetables thrive. Considerable live-stock is raised, and feeding is only done for a few weeks after the 1st of January. At all other times the cattle keep in good condition by grazing. An experiment in hops was tried last year, by planting a few acres about half a mile from the tide-lands, with so satisfactory results that it will be repeated on a larger scale.

The so-called "Olympian Marshes" are situated about 6 miles from La Conner. These marshes are subject to the overflow of the Skagit when the stream is swollen, but they may be reclaimed by diking. Their area is at least 20,000 acres, and they are called beaver-dam lands. There is no question that they would yield on an average 100 bushels of oats to the acre.

Situated along the course of the Skagit, and for a distance of 30 miles from its mouth, are ten lumber camps, comprising the most active logging interests at present on Puget Sound.

On the Skagit, gold, iron and coal have been discovered. About 30 miles from La Conner a valuable coal mine exists, the quality being not unlike that of Cumberland coal. Near the same place rich iron ore has been found, but as yet neither industry has been developed, for lack of capital.

The Saak River, one of the tributaries of the Skagit, flowing into the latter about 50 miles from its mouth, is, in course of time, destined to support a large population. There are 20,000 acres of prairie there on which the Indians now pasture their horses. Already a few whites have gone into this region. East of the Saak the land is comparatively unexplored. The climate is mild, the lands low and level, with growths of vine-maple and alder. The Saak valley extends to the Cascade Mountains, and the Indians object to settlers entering it.

On the Samish River, about 15 miles north of La Conner, there is a fine body of good timber-land. This stream is small, and navigable only for a short distance. Near the mouth there are about 1,500 acres, chiefly tide-lands, under cultivation, and there are settlements extending up the stream for about five miles.

The Chuckanut range of mountains comes abruptly down to the water above the Samish River. They offer the finest kind of sandstone known to the coast. As yet this stone has not been quarried to a great extent. Some public buildings at Seattle and at Port Townsend and at Portland have been built of it, however. This stone is easily worked, and the quantity is inexhaustible.

North of the Chuckanut Mountains, about six miles, is Bellingham Bay, into which flows the Nooksahk River. The county-seat of Whatcom County is at Bellingham Bay, which is one of the finest harbors on the coast, capable of floating and giving secure anchorage to the largest vessels, being sheltered by mountains from the prevailing south-west winds. The town of Whatcom is situated near the mouth of the Nooksahk, and was the seat of the coal mines at Bellingham Bay. These mines were opened in 1854, but suspended operation in 1877.

The Nooksahk River is navigable for a distance of 30 miles by light draught steamers, and for canoes, 30 miles further. At present, log-jams prevent steamers from ascending higher. The Nooksahk Valley is one of the most promising valleys on the Sound, preferable to the Skagit for poorer settlers, inasmuch as the land and river bottoms are above tide-water, and need no diking. The valley extends in a level plateau, running north to the Fraser River, B. C. The territory between the Nooksahk and the Fraser is about 20 miles wide, and from the Cascade Mountains to Bellingham Bay about 25 miles wide. Perhaps one-half of this region is good arable land, and not one-tenth of it is settled.

This country is adapted to general farming and fruit-growing. Apples, pears and peaches of good quality are raised, as well as vegetables of all kinds.

On the west side of the Nooksahk River there is a reservation of 17 sections of land, nearly 11,000 acres, belonging to the Lummi tribe of Indians, who number 400. This land is considered the best in the country.

The population in the Nooksahk country, from Bellingham Bay to the boundary line, is estimated at 1,000. At Whatcom, there is excellent water-power, capable of running large factories.

Semiahmoo Bay, on the Gulf of Georgia, near the boundary line, the terminus of the Sound and Port Townsend steam mail route, is settled by about 75 families, who are engaged in farming and stock-raising.

Fidalgo Island, also in Whatcom County, is perhaps second to Whidby Island in respect to size, population and production. It is close to the main shore. The soil is a good upland, producing excellent hay, vegetables and garden produce. There are also sheep-farms, and the wool is of a good kind.

Guemes Island, San Juan County, east of Rosario Straits, is also of large size. The soil is good, and crops of about the same character are raised as those on Fidalgo Island. There are about 50 families settled here.

Orcas Island, also in San Juan County, lying north-west of Guemes, is mountainous. Valuable silver quartz has recently been discovered on it. Its settlers, about 100 in number, are engaged in stock-raising and general farming.

Lopez Island, San Juan County, is a better island than Orcas, and is nearly as large. There are about 150 settlers engaged in agriculture and sheep husbandry.

San Juan Island, and numerous smaller islands of the group, have large tracts of good prairie land. Attention is given to sheep-raising, the wool being of excellent quality. There are about 250 inhabitants.

Whidby Island, with the adjacent island of Cameno, forms Island County. Whidby is about 60 miles long, and varies greatly in width, being five or six miles at its widest part. It is one of the oldest settlements on Puget Sound. The soil is good, and may be described as a fine upland prairie. There are large bodies of timber on both the northern and southern portions of the island. On Cameno Island, at Utsaladdy, there is a large saw-mill. The population of these two islands is about 1,000.

OTHER REGIONS WORTH LOOKING AFTER.

Large areas of good farming territory remain unsettled, and for the most part unsurveyed, in what is known as the "Colville Country," lying west of the Pend d'Oreille Division of the Northern Pacific Railroad and north of Spokane Falls. The following outline of this region was made in November, 1881, by Indian Agent James O'Neil, and is presented for the information of intending settlers:

"From Spokane Falls to Colville by the Cottonwood Road, running a little west of north, about 45 miles of timbered country is passed through. This timber is mostly pine, with some white pine and considerable tamarack. The soil after it has been cleared is very good. The Colville Valley is entered at Che-we-lah, or Fool's Prairie, where there is a school district and election precinct of 50 voters. The farming portion of the valley from this point to the mouth of the Colville River is about 40 miles long, and from one to three miles wide. Adjoining are other good lands, thinly timbered, which are suitable for grazing, the soil being excellent for agricultural purposes also after it is cleared. For this whole distance the crops of wheat, oats and vegetables will compare favorably with those raised south of the Spokane River. From the mouth of the Colville River to the mouth of the Spokane, the distance is from 45 to 50 miles. On the east bank of the Columbia River are good farming and grazing lands, with capabilities for one hundred and fifty more large farms; the lands immediately upon the Columbia producing excellent corn and other grain, melons, tomatoes, fruit, and vegetables. There are here some Indian farms, but as yet only a few farms occupied by whites, the land being still unsurveyed. Many desirable farms may yet be had in the Columbia Valley, from five to eight miles from Fort Colville in a southeastwardly direction. Towards Pend d'Oreille Lake lies the "White Mud Lake Country," which is still unsurveyed. Many good farms may be taken up in this country. Hundreds of horses winter in this region without care, sustaining themselves on the bunch-grass. Here, too, are numerous fine ledges of marble, white and variegated. In the Colville Valley, also, from Walker Prairie to Che-we-lah, are to be found many ridges of the finest limestone and granite. From Che-we-lah in a southeastwardly direction, a trail, extensively traveled, leads to Kalispel and Pend d'Oreille Lake, distant 35 miles, where the Indians have a few farms. On the west bank of the Columbia, opposite old Fort Colville, and up the Kettle River and on the high lands bordering the British Columbia line, are fine and extensive farming and grazing lands. The whole country is well watered with the purest water in the world, entirely free from alkali. A fine gold-bearing quartz country is being opened about five miles from Che-we-lah, extending some 30 miles towards Spokane Falls, and over toward Lake Pend d'Oreille."

Respecting the mineral resources of this "Colville Country," the U. S. Surveyor General of Washington Territory, W. McMicken, Esq., under date of November 9, 1881, wrote:

"The mineral country, which is locally known as the 'Colville and Wenatchee countries,' may be described as follows:

"The Colville country lies east and west of the Colville Guide meridian, which is extended north between range 39 and 40 east to the north boundary of township 36. This belt extends east across the Clark's Fork of the Columbia and west across the Columbia to the Cascade Mountains. South on the west side of the Columbia to the upper Yakima or Klee-al-um Lake, is the 'Wenatchee country.'

"The rock formation is granite, slate and quartz, and the limited examinations which have been made show that gold, silver and galena exist, not only in paying quantities, but in several localities to great extent and richness. While in the Colville country last September I noticed that many of the small streams ran over quartz pebbles, and granite and slate were visible on all the hillsides along the Colville Valley, also broken fragments of quartz.

"This portion of the territory is unsurveyed and as yet almost unexplored. On the tributaries of the Wenatchee several promising gold mines have been found which are now being developed, and another year will bring to notice rich lodes of silver-bearing rock in the Colville country north of the Spokane River."

In reference to this same region, Major Truax, who for years has been surveying Government lands in Washington Territory and is familiar with the country generally, said:

"From Cheney, on the Northern Pacific Railroad, there is a belt of land about 40 miles wide and over 100 miles in length, bordering the Spokane and Columbia Rivers, which I consider the finest grain country of its size in the Columbia basin. Four-fifths of this is good agricultural land, and the remainder a fine grazing region. These lands are slightly rolling and are thickly covered with bunch-grass, sunflowers and other wild flowers of many varieties, indicating a very rich soil. Settlers are now locating there, even so far distant as 75 miles from the Northern Pacific Railroad, being confident that a branch railroad must soon be built to open up so fine a region, and rather waiting in hope of future advantage than locating on poorer land nearer the railroad. Perhaps two or three hundred pioneers have settled here in the course of 1881."

THE NORTHERN PACIFIC RAILROAD AND OTHER LANDS.

The bulk of the agricultural lands of the Northern Pacific Railroad, in the Pacific North-west, now in market, is situated in Yakima, Walla Walla, Columbia, Garfield, Whitman and Stevens Counties, Washington Territory, and in Nez Percé County, Idaho. These lands are, for the most part, accessible, and within easy reach of transportation facilities, not only by way of the trunk line of the Northern Pacific Railroad and the Columbia and Snake Rivers, but also by the branches of the Oregon Railway and Navigation Company's system, extending from Walla Walla over the region south of Snake River, and from a point on the line of the Northern Pacific, 48 miles north-east of Ainsworth, through the territory watered by the Palouse and its numerous tributaries. Among the

COMMERCIAL STREET, SEATTLE, W. T.

regions most desirable for settlement may be mentioned those watered by Crab, Rock and Hangman Creeks, in Stevens County, and by Thorne, Pine and Cottonwood Creeks, in Whitman County. The soil is exceedingly rich and productive, and living water is found on almost every quarter-section. There are also extensive tracts of equally desirable railroad land in the Counties of Garfield, Columbia, Yakima and Walla Walla.

The lands of the Northern Pacific Railroad, lying west of the Cascade Mountains, are principally timbered. There are, however, large tracts in the valleys of the Chehalis, Cowlitz, Lewis and Salmon Rivers as well as on the plateau north of the Columbia, extending toward the Cascade Mountains, which may be easily cleared and brought under cultivation. Here, all kinds of fruit and grain thrive equally well. On Puget Sound, too, there is plenty of rich bottom land that can be brought under cultivation at but little cost.

The Northern Pacific Railroad Company sells it lands on easy terms, and at low prices, assisting intending settlers in every way to find suitable locations.

Besides the Northern Pacific Railroad Company and the United States Government, the Oregon Improvement Company is the largest seller of land in the territory east of the Cascade Mountains. This company owns 145,000 acres of carefully selected agricultural land in Whitman County, Washington Territory, and 20,000 acres in Grande Ronde and Powder River valleys, Baker County, Oregon. These lands are particularly desirable, owing to their proximity to the Palouse branches, and the Grande Ronde branch of the Oregon Railway and Navigation Company. They are sold on easy terms, at from $5 to $10 per acre.

THE UNITED STATES LAND LAWS.

The liberal provisions which have been made by the United States Government for acquiring public lands are to be found in the following summary of the acts of Congress relating to the subject :

Under the provisions of the "Homestead Law," every head of a family, male or female, or single man over twenty-one years of age, a citizen of the United States, or having declared his intention to become such, can enter, on payment of the registry fees, which range from $5.50 to $22, one hundred and sixty acres of Government land, excepting lands bearing gold, silver, cinnabar or copper. After five years' continuous residence upon and improvement of the land, the Government will give the claimant a perfect title.

Under the Pre-emption Law, persons who are qualified to take up land under the conditions applying to the homestead law, and who are not already in possession of three hundred and twenty acres in any of the States or Territories of the United States, may "enter" and establish a pre-emption right, at the Government Land Office of the district, on payment of a fee of $3. In other words, any such person has the right to purchase a tract of one hundred and sixty acres, either within or without the limits of a railroad grant, at $2.50 per acre in the former, and at $1.25 per acre in the latter case. Where the tract is offered for sale by the Government, the land must be paid for within thirteen months from the date of settlement, otherwise within thirty-three months.

Under the Timber Culture Act one hundred and sixty acres is the maximum entry. This act is liberal in its provisions, but claimants are required to strictly comply with the letter and spirit of its terms. During the first year at least five acres must be ploughed. The second year said five acres must be actually cultivated to crop, and a second five acres ploughed. The third year the first five acres must be planted in timber, seeds, or cuttings, and the second five acres actually cultivated to crop. The fourth year the second five acres must be planted in timber, seeds, or cuttings, making, at the end of the fourth year, ten acres thus planted. Perfect good faith must be shown at all times by claimants. The timber must not only be planted, but it must each year be protected and cultivated in such a manner as to promote its growth. A patent may be obtained for the land at the expiration of eight years from date of entry, upon showing that for said eight years the trees have been planted, protected and cultivated as aforesaid, *and that not less than* 2,700 *trees were planted on each acre,* and at the time of making proof there shall be then growing at least 675 *living, thrifty trees to each acre.* If at any time during the said eight years it shall be shown that the party has failed to comply with the terms of the law, the entry will be canceled. Only the planting of such trees, seeds, or cuttings as are properly denominated timber trees, or which are recognized as forest trees, will be considered a compliance with the law. Cottonwood is recognized as timber under the act. All entries of less than one quarter section shall be ploughed, planted, cultivated and planted to trees, tree seeds, or cuttings, in the same manner and in the proportion hereinbefore provided for in the one hundred and sixty acre entry. The Land Office fee for an entry of more than eighty acres is $14; for one of eighty acres or less, $9.

The United States Land Offices in Oregon are situated at Oregon City, Roseburg, The Dalles, La Grande and Linkville, and those in Washington Territory are to be found at Olympia, Vancouver, Yakima City, Walla Walla and Colfax. At each of these offices the usual facilities to settlers who wish to take up Government lands are offered.

TAXATION.

Oregon has earned a good reputation for economy in Government expenditures, and the rate of taxation is extremely moderate. The legislative appropriations for all purposes connected with the State during the two years ended September, 1880, were $395,952. The receipts of the State Treasurer for the same period were $432,605, this amount being derived principally from a four mill tax. The estimated expenditures of the State for the two years ending September, 1882, are put at $354,280. The disbursements include interest on the bonded debt of the State, which amounted, on September 1, 1880, to $511,376, a large part of which was incurred during the Modoc and Umatilla Indian wars, and for which a claim has been made upon the Government of the United States. According to the national census of 1880 the total assessed value of real and personal property in the State was $69,754,113, divided as follows : land and improvements, $53,723,643; farm machinery and tools, $2,913,750; live stock, $13,116,720. It may, however, be taken for granted that the real worth of the property exceeded by at least one-half the figures here given. Assessors rarely comply with the statute which requires that taxes shall be levied upon property at its full cash value. Complaints of unjust assessment are heard before boards of equalization.

Washington Territory, since 1879, has only imposed a tax of three mills on the dollar. The Territory, at the close of September, 1881, was entirely free from debt, and had a cash balance in the treasury of $22,715. This favorable condition of the finances was due to the steady and healthful increase of property valuations during the years 1880 and 1881, and to the economy exercised with respect to appropriations and expenditures. The assessed value of all property in 1881 was $25,786,415, and the territorial tax levy on the same was $77,351. Taking these figures as a basis, and assuming that the rate of increase will not diminish, it is estimated that during the ensuing two years the gross amount of territorial tax, at the rate of three mills on the dollar, will reach the sum of about $150,000 to meet the current expenses of the period ending September 30, 1883.

COMMERCE.

For many years Oregon and Washington Territory were commercially dependent upon California. Gradually, however (and just in the ratio of increase of the productions of the region), commercial independence has been achieved. Exportations of wheat, flour, salmon and other staples are no longer made so largely through the medium of San Francisco. Neither are supplies drawn from that quarter to the same extent as was formerly the case. Portland now buys merchandise not only in all the great cities of the United States, but also directly in foreign markets. The same is true of Astoria and other centres of business. The commerce of the country has become self-sustaining, because production has been stimulated by the opening of lines of transportation.

From statistics carefully prepared at the Custom Houses at Portland and Astoria the following facts are given to show the volume of the foreign trade. The direct exports of domestic products from the Columbia River to foreign ports during the years 1880 and 1881, were :

FROM PORTLAND.

	1880.	Value.
Wheat,	1,762,515 bushels	$1,845,537
Flour,	180,763 barrels	891,872
	Total	$2,737,409

	1881.	Value.
Wheat,	4,076,508 bushels	$3,765,232
Flour,	337,395 barrels	1,484,311
Other merchandise		74,960
	Total	$5,324,503

SPOKANE FALLS, W. T.

FROM ASTORIA.

1880.		Value.
Wheat,	479,721 bushels	$469,032
Flour,	17,894 barrels	86,779
Salmon,	204,855 cases	1,022,157
Other merchandise		3,147
	Total	$1,581,115

1881.		Value.
Wheat,	790,510 bushels	$739,170
Flour,	49,652 barrels	248,852
Salmon,	342,149 cases	1,736,993
	Total	$2,724,915

By comparing the foregoing figures it will be seen that the aggregate value of domestic exports from the Columbia River to foreign countries has nearly doubled in the short space of one year—the actual increase being $3,730,894, and that the grand total of direct foreign shipments during the two years was $12,367,742.

The bulk of the exports of wheat and flour is shipped to England, Ireland, Belgium and France. Salmon goes almost exclusively to England.

The increase of the business with China is quite marked. In 1880, the value of merchandise imported from Hong-Kong was $84,808, and in 1881 it was $137,234. Eventually a large portion of the trade of the Pacific coast with China must fall to Portland. The mouth of the Columbia is several days' sailing nearer to the chief Chinese ports than is the Golden Gate, and when direct railroad communication to Eastern ports is open the trade will naturally be diverted to the shortest route.

It must be kept in mind that the foregoing facts and figures apply only to the direct foreign trade. Statistics of the coastwise business are not embraced therein. Portland alone exports every few days, by steamship, to San Francisco large quantities of wheat, flour, wool, cattle, fish, and other commodities.

Attempts are constantly made to injure the commerce of Portland and Astoria by exaggerated reports of the dangers connected with the bar at the entrance to the Columbia River. It is, however, a fact, that the passage of vessels over the bar is not attended with more danger than that incident to entering the ports of San Francisco or New York. This truth has been confirmed at various times by official investigations and reports. At high water, ships of the greatest draught, and at low water, vessels drawing seventeen feet, can easily enter the river and proceed to the well-built wharves of Portland.

The constant increase of the shipping business at Portland and Astoria affords the best evidence that the bar is no obstruction to navigation. For instance, in 1880, there cleared at the Custom Houses of Portland and Astoria 141 vessels, aggregating 213,143 tons measurement. Of these, 93 vessels, measuring 172,532 tons, were engaged in the coastwise, and the remaining 48, measuring 40,611 tons, were employed in the foreign trade. In 1881 the clearances of vessels for foreign ports from Portland alone were not less than 140, with a total measurement of 130,000 tons, and the clearances for coastwise ports, including the steamships of the Oregon Railway and Navigation Company, for San Francisco, were not short of 100, making a total of 240 clearances for the year, or an increase of 100 seagoing vessels, as compared with the clearances of 1880.

MEANS OF COMMUNICATION.

The navigable water-courses of the country, so numerous and so important to its welfare, have been elsewhere described. Great benefits must always be derived from these natural highways. They will not only be an auxiliary to the artificial channels of transportation, but in many instances will enter into lively competition with them. Upon the latter, however, the region must chiefly depend for opening up the great expanses of fertile lands to profitable agriculture and for affording opportunities to develop the mining and other dormant resources. The fact is patent that railway enterprise is wonderfully active at present in Oregon and Washington Territory. The locomotive is literally preparing the way for settlement and civilization, instead of following in their train. Railroads now tap the fruitful valleys of the Columbia, the Willamette and the Snake Rivers, and are rapidly reaching out to other wheat-producing regions. By these means remote districts have already been brought into direct connection with Portland and San Francisco, and ready transportation will soon be given to the largest surplus of products. Immigrants, also, may now travel continuously by speedy and comfortable conveyances, to the homes and farms which they wish to possess. The long and tedious journey by wagon roads, with its train of hardships and dangers, is numbered with past events, and a rich and smiling country, so long hidden in solitude, is now revealed to the world and invites to occupation. Within the space of a short two years, also, this valuable part of our broad domain will be brought into direct intercourse with the Eastern States by means of the Northern Pacific Railroad, the construction of which verges rapidly to its close. This great enterprise in successful operation, no element will be lacking to secure the rapid advancement of the Pacific North-west to lasting prosperity.

The names of the several railway and steamship lines are as follows:

1. The Northern Pacific Railroad, from Wallula Junction, in Washington Territory, to Lake Pend d'Oreille, in Idaho (233 miles). The road traverses for the most part a fine agricultural country in Whitman and Stevens Counties, W. T., and also richly timbered and mining region in Kootenai County, Idaho, rendering them available to settlers and industrial enterprise.

2. Pacific Division of the same railroad, extending from Kalama, on the Columbia River, to Tacoma, on Puget Sound (105 miles), with a branch line (30 miles) to the coal regions of Wilkeson and Carbonado. This road passes through a most interesting part of Washington Territory.

3. A short narrow-gauge railroad from Olympia to Tenino, on the line of the Pacific Division of the Northern Pacific Railroad.

4. The Oregon and California Railroad (East-side Division), from East Portland to Roseburg, in the Umpqua Valley, a distance of two hundred miles. The road follows the east side of the Willamette and touches all the principal towns in the valley. Its extension to the California line is now in progress. From Roseburg a well-managed stage line runs to Redding, in the Sacramento Valley (180 miles), the present northern terminus of the California railroad system.

5. The Oregon and California Railroad (West-side Division), beginning at Portland, within the city limits, and following the west side of the Willamette River,

Passing westwardly through Washington County, it then turns to the south and ends at Corvallis (97 miles). This line will be extended to Junction City, some miles further, to unite with the Oregon and California Railroad, and eventually, also, in a northwest direction to Astoria, at the mouth of the Columbia River.

6. The Oregon Railway Company, limited, a narrow-gauge road, also traverses the most fertile lands of the Willamette Valley, on both sides of the river. This line flanks the Oregon and California Railroad. It begins at Coburg 120 miles from Portland, on the east side of the river and skirts the foot-hills, running north until it approaches Ray's Landing. It continues its course on the west side of the valley, running south to Airlie, a distance of 37 miles, with a branch of 7 miles to Sheridan. This line has been leased to the Oregon Railway and Navigation Company.

7. The Oregon Railway and Navigation Company's Railroad. A standard gauge line, fully equipped, running from Portland mainly through the valley of the Columbia River, by way of The Dalles, to Wallula, thence to Walla Walla and Dayton, with a branch from Bolles' Junction to Texas Ferry, on the Snake River. There is also a narrow-gauge branch from Whitman, near Walla Walla, to Blue Mountain Station, near Weston, in Oregon.

8. The ocean steamship lines of the same company, being a fleet of first-class passenger and freight steamships, making regular trips every five days between San Francisco and Portland, as well as forming a line between San Francisco, British Columbia, the ports on Puget Sound and Alaska.

. 9. A fleet of 30 river steamboats and barges, plying daily on the Lower, Middle and Upper Columbia and Snake and Willamette Rivers, traversing the last-named river to the head of its navigable waters ; together with the steamboats and facilities formerly owned by the Willamette Locks and Transportation Company.

10. The fleet of four new iron steam colliers, comprising the *Mississippi,* the *Umatilla,* the *Willamette* and the *Walla Walla,* which make frequent trips between Seattle and San Francisco.

Appended are the routes of travel which now radiate from Portland, with the mileage in operation :

Willamette Valley Routes :

	MILES.
From Portland to Roseberg, by the Oregon and California Railroad	200
From Albany to Lebanon, by the Oregon and California Railroad	9
From Portland to Corvallis, by the Oregon and California Railroad	97
From Portland to Coburg, by the narrow gauge division of the Oregon Railway and Navigation Company	120
From Portland to Airlie, by the narrow gauge division of the Oregon Railway and Navigation Company	37
From Airlie to Sheridan, branch of last-named road	7
From Portland to Dayton, by Oregon Railway and Navigation Company's steamboats	45
From Portland to Corvallis, by Oregon Railway and Navigation Company's steamboats	115

Lower Columbia Route :

From Portland to Astoria, by Oregon Railway and Navigation Company's steamboats	98

Puget Sound Route :

From Portland to Kalama, by Oregon Railway and Navigation Company's steamboats	38
From Kalama to Tacoma, by Northern Pacific Railroad (Pacific Division)	105
From Tacoma to Carbonado, by Northern Pacific Railroad (Pacific Division)	30
From Tacoma to Victoria, B. C., by Oregon Railway and Navigation Company's steamboats	120

	MILES.
From Seattle to La Conner, by Oregon Railway and Navigation Company's steamboats	55
From Seattle to Newcastle, by the Columbia and Puget Sound Narrow Gauge Railroad	22

Upper Columbia Route:

	MILES.
From Portland to The Dalles, by the Oregon Railway and Navigation Company's railroad or steamboats	110
From The Dalles to Wallula Junction, by the Oregon Railway and Navigation Company's railway	126
From Wallula Junction to Walla Walla, by the Oregon Railway and Navigation Company's railway	34
From Walla Walla to Texas Ferry, by the Oregon Railway and Navigation Company's railway	56
From Bolles' Junction to Dayton, by the Oregon Railway and Navigation Company's railway	14
From Whitman to Blue Mountain Station, by the Oregon Railway and Navigation Company's railway (narrow gauge)	14
From Texas Ferry to Lewiston, on Snake River, by the Oregon Railway and Navigation Company's steamboats	78
From Wallula Junction to Lake Pend d'Oreille, by the Northern Pacific Railroad (Pend d'Oreille Division)	233

Ocean Routes:

From Portland to San Francisco, by the Oregon Railway and Navigation Company's steamships	670
From San Francisco to Victoria, B. C., and Puget Sound ports, by Oregon Railway and Navigation Company and Oregon Improvement Company's steamships	800
Total in operation	3,233

In addition to which are the following projected lines of railroad now in course of construction by the Oregon Railway and Navigation Company:

	MILES.
Columbia River to Grande Ronde Valley, in process of construction	170
From a point 148 miles north-east of Ainsworth, on the main line of the Northern Pacific Railroad, to Colfax, located, work about to commence	64
Pataha and Lewiston Branch, located, work about to commence	66
Farmington and Pine Creek Branch, located, work about to commence	45
Moscow Branch, located, work about to commence	25
Elk Creek Branch, located, work about to commence	16
Total projected and to be completed	386
Add total in operation	3,233
Total completed and projected	3,619

In this connection it should be mentioned that the Oregon Railway and Navigation Company, and also the Northern Pacific Railroad Company, have adopted the policy of fixing a uniform low rate of freight from all points east of Umatilla in transporting the products of the country. Thus the farmers and grain-producers at remote points on the line of railroad extensions obtain the same prices for their shipments as those who are nearer the market.

OREGON RAILWAY AND NAVIGATION COMPANY'S DOCK (900 FEET LONG), PORTLAND, OREGON.

APPENDIX.

DESCRIPTION OF COUNTIES.

Subjoined will be found, in merest outline, a summary of the leading facts connected with the several counties, with regard to their area, settlement, population in 1880, products, industries, topography, etc., which may serve intended settlers in making a choice of location.

OREGON.

BAKER COUNTY,

in Eastern Oregon, lies south of Union and east of Grant. It is nearly 200 miles long and 100 broad. Population, 4,615. Area, 10,183,680 acres; surveyed, 1,702,000 ; unsurveyed, 8,481,680; settled, 437,584. Baker City is the county seat. In the mountains are rich deposits of gold and silver, and the mines are worked to advantage. There are many fertile valleys, among which may be named the Powder and Burnt River valleys, producing large crops of grain and vegetables. In addition are immense bunch-grass and sage-bush tracts, which will eventually be brought under the plough, only requiring irrigation in many places to make them productive. At present the unoccupied lands are used as grazing grounds. There are about 50,000 head of cattle herded in the county. Much attention is paid to horse-breeding, and the animals bred here are among the best produced in the State. The value of live stock is estimated at $1,000,000, and the farm productions last year amounted to over $250,000. Among the products are butter, cheese, wool, barley, corn, oats, rye, wheat, potatoes, apples and peaches. The county indebtedness in 1881 was $30,000, and the taxable property $1,000,000, having increased one-half in five years. As soon as the railroad now in course of rapid construction is completed, this county will be in direct communication with Portland, and fine opportunities will be opened to settlers.

BENTON COUNTY,

in Western Oregon, lies south of Polk, and is bounded on the west by the Pacific Ocean. Population, 6,403. Area, 1,197,000 acres; surveyed, 737,000; unsurveyed, 460,000 ; settled, 322,000. It takes in Yaquina Bay, the harbor of which is adapted to light-draught vessels. Corvallis, the county seat, is also the terminus of the West Side Division of the Oregon and California Railroad, tapping the west side of the Willamette Valley. The surface of the country is varied. The valley lands produce largely, the wheat crop in 1880 amounting to 486,000 bushels. Estimated

value of all farm products, $638,000. Besides the growing of wheat, much atten-
tion is paid to dairying, sheep-raising and fruit culture. Monroe and Philomath
are important towns. The State Agricultural College, established at Corvallis, is
in a prosperous condition. There is considerable arable land in the county, particularly in the western part, which may be taken up or bought cheaply from either
the railroad or the State University.

CLACKAMAS COUNTY,

in Western Oregon, lies south of Multnomah and mainly east of the Willamette
River. Population, 9,260. Area, 920,000 acres; surveyed, 460,000; unsurveyed,
460,000; settled, 345,000. The surface of the country is chiefly hilly, with only
occasional open land. The soil of the foot-hills, after it is cleared, is of the best
quality, and offers great inducements to the settler. This land, when summer
fallowed, yields 25 bushels of wheat per acre. Sheep-raising prospers, and there
are fine woolen factories, which not only supply the home demand, but export
their cloths and blankets to California. Oregon City, the county seat, is the largest
town in the county and the oldest in the State, and has immense water-power
facilities.

CLATSOP COUNTY

lies in the north-west corner of the State. Population, 7,222. Area, 552,000 acres;
surveyed, 207,000; unsurveyed, 345,000; settled, 115,000. Nineteen-twentieths
of its surface are covered with timber, chiefly cedar, spruce, hemlock, white and
yellow fir, the latter being most valuable and most plentiful. The lumber business of the county is large and prosperous. One saw-mill at Astoria cuts 6.000.000
feet annually, much of which is used in making cases for salmon-packing. Astoria, the principal town and county seat, is situated twelve miles from the mouth
of the Columbia River, and possesses great advantages as a shipping and commer-
cial·port. It has in its precinct 3,981 inhabitants, and during the salmon-fishing
season the number is increased to about 6,000 by the laborers and fishermen. Its
water-front is good, and its wharves are kept in excellent order. Some idea of the
trade of the place may be gained from the fact that its shipments of lumber, wheat,
flour, salmon, etc., in 1881, amounted to nearly $3,000,000. Salmon-canning is
the principal industry of the county. There are eighteen canning establishments,
representing a large capital. Fruit is put up during the winter in some of these
canneries, and this business should increase. A tannery in Upper Astoria has
been quite successful, and a boot and shoe factory in connection with it is quite
prosperous. The climate is not adapted to fruit growing, save for certain varieties
of apples and plums, the quality of which could not be excelled. Near Saddle
Mountain good coal fields have been found. The county offers fair advantages
to the immigrant. Its surface is well watered, and the equable climate makes it
a great summer resort.

COLUMBIA COUNTY

lies east of Clatsop. Population, 2,042. Area, 368,000 acres; surveyed, 299,000;
unsurveyed, 69,000; settled, 115,000. There are good farming lands on the banks
of the Klaskanie River, and some small settlements in the valleys, a considerable
one being at Oak Point, on the Columbia. At Riverside, on the Nehalem River,

is a colony of Scandinavians, who prefer the wooded, hilly country to prairie-land. These people have cleared off the timber and now have good farms. On the east side of the county, nearer Portland, are rich farms and thick settlements.

COOS COUNTY

is situated west of Douglas County. Population, 4,834. It has been for thirty-five years the seat of a profitable trade in coal and lumber, and it also has a fur business amounting to about $10,000 per year. On the Coos River there is good agricultural land, and the area might be indefinitely enlarged if the tide-marshes were diked. The coal interest is quite important. The yield is large and turns in a fine revenue to the county, maintaining a line of steamers between Coos Bay and San Francisco. An extensive lumber business is also carried on. At Marshfield there is a ship-yard employing 25 men, and the saw-mill at the same place cuts 1,000,000 feet per month. Another mill at South Bend saws 700,000 feet per month, and gives occupation to 50 men, inclusive of those employed in a ship-yard connected with it. Each year two or three vessels are launched. The county has unoccupied, and mainly unsurveyed, lands enough to support at least 50,000 people. There are fine grazing lands in the county, and its annual production of butter and cheese alone exceeds 100,000 pounds. It exports wool, and produces corn, wheat, oats, potatoes and apples in paying crops. With the exception of peaches, fruits thrive excellently.

CURRY COUNTY

in the south-west corner of the State, on the California line, is very thinly populated, the last census showing only 1,208 inhabitants. Its area is mainly mountainous, and only a tithe of it has been surveyed. The people support themselves by sheep-raising, dairying, lumbering, fishing and placer mining. The arable land under cultivation produces sufficiently for home consumption, and the total value of farm productions is set down at $69,000.

DOUGLAS COUNTY

lies in south-western Oregon. Population, 9,596. Area, 3,710,000 acres, only one-half of which has been surveyed, and only 690,000 acres are occupied. The country is well watered, and the valleys of the Umpqua River and its tributaries are remarkably fruitful. Every sort of vegetable known in the temperate zone, the cereals and all the fruits, excepting peaches, yield in abundance. The county is noted for its sheep. The wool is of the finest quality. In 1880, Douglas County shipped 1,000,000 pounds of wool and drove 27,000 sheep into Nevada. The yield of wheat is set down at 441,000 bushels ; of apples, at 257,000 bushels ; of oats, at 347,000 bushels, and 280,000 pounds of butter and cheese. About 800 hides are annually tanned in the Umpqua Valley. The chief business on the lower Umpqua River is lumbering. There is a good harbor at the mouth of the stream for small vessels, which transport the lumber to San Francisco. The product per year amounts to about 3,000,000 feet, and $300,000 are disbursed during the same period for labor and material. Salmon-canning is also an important business. There are two establishments on the river which put up about 10,000 cases. In educational advantages, Douglas County keeps up to the mark. Each district has at least one school term in the year. Umpqua Academy, at Wilbur, is one of the oldest educational establishments in the State, and is a first-class school. There are several flourishing towns in the county. Of these, the principal is Roseburg, with a population of 822. This place is the southern terminus of the Oregon and California Railroad, distant from Portland 200 miles, and is the shipping and distributing centre of Southern Oregon. There are churches of almost every denomination, and many fine residences and large business establishments. Considerable gold-mining is carried on in several localities. The climate is mild and equable, and admits of out-door work throughout the year.

GRANT COUNTY

is in Eastern Oregon, lying east of Wasco and Lake Counties, and extending to the Blue Mountain Range. Population, 4,303. Area, 9,640,000 acres; surveyed, 1,260,000; unsurveyed, 8,380,000; settled, 191,000. Formerly, the rich placer mines of the John Day River and other streams supported an active population. and caused a brisk trade, but these placers are now nearly worked out. Quartz-mining at present offers encouragement to enterprise, and will eventually prove a source of permanent prosperity. The prominent business of the county is herding and horse-breeding, there being extensive pasture ranges for herds and flocks. The cultivated lands produce largely, and there will shortly be a great addition to the agricultural area of the State by opening the tract known as the Malheur Indian Reservation to settlement, the aborigines having been removed. The county lies remote from present railway enterprises, but sheep and cattle ranchmen find it an excellent region for their purposes.

JACKSON COUNTY

is situated in Western Oregon, south of Douglas. Population, 8,154. Its area is about 3,000 square miles, or over 3,000,000 acres, one-third of which is fine prairie land. Its principal valley is that of the Rogue River, which is 43 miles long. and in places 22 miles wide. The climate is as agreeable as that of central and northern California. Every garden vegetable thrives. Fruits of all kinds are raised quite easily, and peaches of fine quality yield bountifully. Excellent grapes are produced. On all the bottom-lands wheat, barley, oats, rye and corn are produced in astonishing and unfailing crops, some of the farms yielding as high as 25 bushels of wheat per acre after a score of years of continued cultivation. Corn is the second crop in importance. There are five flour-mills in the county, and at Ashland a woolen-mill makes very good cloth. The business of making wine and brandy has been fairly begun, and promises to develop satisfactorily. The stock business is also of great importance, as the animals may be easily driven to market. Mining, however, is the great industry. All the mines now worked are placers, and they yield largely. There are also fine quartz ledges, which await capital to develop them. Jacksonville and Ashland are the principal towns, each with about 850 inhabitants. The former has a public school, a girls' school taught by Sisters of Charity, Presbyterian, Methodist and Catholic Churches; a bank, planing-mill and two newspapers. Ashland has two churches, a Methodist school, a woolen mill, marble works and one newspaper. The timber resources of the county are great, but quite undeveloped. Oak, ash, cedar, alder, yellow fir and other varieties abound, and the forests and streams are full of game. The extension of the

Oregon and California Railroad, which is about to take place, will arouse the entire region into life and prosperity.

JOSEPHINE COUNTY,

lying between Curry and Jackson, in the south-western part of the State, has a population of 2,485. This county is quite mountainous, and is only partially surveyed. The land under cultivation is not more than sufficient to supply the home demand for vegetables and fruit, but there are many valleys which would produce largely. Mining is the principal occupation, but dairying, cattle and sheep-raising receive attention. Its remoteness from transportation lines is a serious drawback to the development of the county. The aggregate value of its farm products scarcely exceeds $100,000.

LAKE COUNTY

lies in the middle of Southern Oregon. Population, 2,804. As its name implies, it is a region of lakes, all of which are of considerable size. The soil is generally light, composed of volcanic ashes. Although a high and frosty county, it has many fine valleys and excellent land. Lake View, on Goose Lake, the county seat, is a thriving town, with two newspapers. Sprague River Valley, quite picturesquely situated, contains 20,000 acres of excellent land, the soil being a rich sandy loam. Linkville, on Klamath Lake, is a good trading centre. Stock-raising is the most prominent business of the county. Only within a recent period have the bunch-grass and sage-bush lands, which here abound, been cultivated, but the result of what was simply an experiment was so encouraging that a broad acreage of cereals will soon be produced.

LANE COUNTY

is situated at the head of the Willamette Valley, and extends from the Cascade Mountains to the Ocean. Population, 9,411. Area, 2,875,000 acres; surveyed, 1,150,000; unsurveyed, 1,725,000; settled, 690,000. The surface is quite diversified. There is much mountain and foot-hill land, and the prairies are extensive and very fertile. In all parts of the county there are large tracts of good land inviting settlers, and especially is this the case in the western part. Fine opportunities are offered also for the stock-raiser. Long-wooled sheep and Devon cattle are successfully bred. Wheat, oats, barley, hops, fruit and vegetables yield well. With ordinary cultivation the wheat crop runs from 25 to 30 bushels per acre. The principal town is Eugene City, which, including the precincts of North and South Eugene, contains a population of 2,250. This town is finely situated and beautifully laid out. It is the seat of the State University, and promises to be the educational centre of the Pacific North-west. Other important places are Goshen, Creswell, Junction City and Springfield.

LINN COUNTY

lies south of Marion and west of the Cascade Mountains. It is the great prairie county of Western Oregon. Population, 12,675. Area, 1,196,000 acres; surveyed, 483,000; unsurveyed, 713,000; settled, 368,000. The soil is rich, yielding often 35 bushels of wheat to the acre. Flax grown here is of fine quality, the fibre being from four to five feet long. Wool is exported heavily, and oats, hay, vegetables and fruit of all kinds are raised. The Oregon and California Railroad and the narrow-gauge road before described, with the Willamette River in addition, give this county excellent transportation facilities. The valleys of the forks of the Santiam River offer fine lands for cultivation. Albany is the county seat, and it is one of the most prosperous towns in the State. Here there is a flax mill for the manufacture of linen twine. Other thriving towns are Tangent, Shedd, Halsey, Peoria, Harrisburg and Brownsville, at which latter place there is a woolen manufactory.

MARION COUNTY

is situated south of Clackamas and east of the Willamette River, extending to the summit of the Cascade Mountains. Population, 14,576. Area, 759,000 acres; surveyed, 529,000; unsurveyed, 230,000; settled, 437,000. The section extending from the foot-hills to the Willamette River is about twenty miles square. It is a good farming district, having been settled years ago. The Waldo Hills are a high rolling prairie, having remarkably fertile soil, and south of these hills Santiam Prairie is also an excellent farming region. Improved farms may be bought at reasonable prices. The transportation facilities are excellent, the Willamette being navigable nearly all the year, the Oregon and California Railroad traversing the valley and the narrow-gauge road skirting the foot-hills. Salem, the capital of the State, is a beautiful town of nearly 5,000 inhabitants, having churches, schools and all social advantages. Willamette University, one of the best colleges on the Pacific Coast, is also situated here. The town has a fine water-power, which is already used to some extent by mills and factories. Some of the principal places are Slayton, Sublimity, Marion, Nehama, Jefferson and Silverton, on the railroads, and Aurora, Gervais and Hubbard.

MULTNOMAH COUNTY

is a narrow strip of country extending from Columbia and Washington Counties along the southern bank of the Columbia River to the Summit of the Cascade Mountains. Population, 26,000. Area, 276,000 acres; surveyed, 161,000; unsurveyed, 115,000; settled, 138,000. The chief city is Portland, which has been described in another place. The county is covered with forests of fir, with some oak, ash and other deciduous trees. Very little farming is done, but market-gardening and dairying are carried on extensively. Strawberries and other fruits are cultivated largely and find ready sale. The scenery about the Columbia River is very grand. The climate is mild, and in summer the nights are always cool. There are, on an average, 237 bright, clear days a year, in spite of the rainy season, which lasts from the middle of October to the middle of April.

POLK COUNTY

lies opposite Marion, on the western bank of the Willamette River, and between Yamhill County on the north and Benton on the south. On the west it is bounded by Tillamook County. Population, 6,601. Area, 414,000 acres; surveyed, 275,000; unsurveyed, 139,000; settled, 230,000. The surface of the county is greatly diversified, a densely-wooded section of the Coast Range, with rolling hills and rich bottom-lands, forming its natural features. It is well watered. The Luckiamute River, a tributary of the Willamette, is navigable for small steamers, and there are many other streams beside, which would supply an almost unlimited water-power to saw and flouring mills. The West Side Division of the Oregon and California Railroad traverses the county. Not far from half the county is timber land, ash, maple, fir, spruce and hemlock being the chief varieties. Dallas, the county seat, has excellent water power, which is utilized largely by mills and factories. There are manufactories of carriages and wagons, household furniture, and doors and sashes, as well as a tannery, a machine shop and a flouring mill. A fine school building has been put up, in which, during a part of the year, an academic course, endowed by a private citizen, is given. Monmouth is also a prosperous town, and is the seat of " The Christian College," an excellent educational establishment, which was founded twenty years ago. The products of the county are wheat, potatoes, oats, hops, cattle, hogs, wool and flour. Apples, pears, plums, cherries, and all sorts of berries, yield bounteously. There is still much good land to be had at prices, for unimproved, varying from $2.50 to $10 per acre.

TILLAMOOK COUNTY

is situated on the coast, lying between Clatsop and Benton Counties. Population, 1,000. Area, 1,012,000 acres; surveyed, 207,000; unsurveyed, 805,000; settled, 115,000. The county seat is Tillamook, situated upon the bay of the same name. In general features this county is similar to Clatsop. Beside lumbering, a good business is done by the people in dairying, for which pursuit the climate and country offer special advantages. The outlet across the coast mountains being difficult, the county is comparatively isolated, its means of communication and transportation being supplied by small vessels. The region is well adapted to sheep-husbandry and stock-raising. Besides Tillamook, the county seat, the principal towns are Nehalem, Garibaldi and Nestockton.

UMATILLA COUNTY,

in Eastern Oregon, lies east of Wasco, on the Columbia River, and is bounded by Grant County on the south, Union County on the east, and the Washington Territory line on the north. Population, 9,607. Area, 4,170,240 acres; surveyed, 1,564,000; unsurveyed, 2,606,240; settled, 1,056,000. West of the Umatilla River stock-raising and sheep husbandry are carried on largely, there being nearly 300,000 head of sheep in 1880. In the north-east part of the county immense quantities of wheat are raised. All along the foot of the Blue Mountains is a stretch of fine arable country, from twenty-five to thirty miles in width. The great productiveness of the soil, and the heavy yield of wheat, have already led to the construction of a branch railroad, 12 miles long, from Whitman to Weston station, and the Grande Ronde branch of the Oregon Railway and Navigation Company's system will also traverse the region a distance of one hundred miles, opening a very fertile part of the county to settlement. The county is well watered, and there are enormous tracts of bunch-grass lands, hitherto used as stock ranges, which must soon be settled and turned into grain fields and orchards. Among these may be mentioned the Cold Spring country, extending along the Columbia River a very considerable distance, and in width about fifteen miles. This section is now attracting attention in view of its deep, rich soil and mild climate, which admits of the cultivation of tobacco, sorghum, corn, tomatoes, and the finer fruits, with little fear of frost. Among the principal places in the county are Pendleton, the county seat, Pilot Rock, Umatilla, Milton, Heppner and Centreville. Timber for building and fencing is supplied by the Blue Mountains, and at Milton it is cheaply brought by a flume from a distance of many miles.

UNION COUNTY

lies east of Umatilla County, and is a very attractive region. Population, 6,650. Area, 3,456,000 acres; surveyed, 894,000; unsurveyed, 2,562,000; settled, 577,000. Being sheltered by the Blue Mountains on the west, the climate is quite mild and healthy. The Grande Ronde Valley, particularly described elsewhere, is traversed by the newly-constructed line of the Oregon Railway and Navigation Company, which brings this fertile and delightful region in railroad connection with points East and West. The principal industry has been stock-raising, sheep-farming, horse-breeding and dairying. A great deal of butter is made, and pork is also largely produced for the Idaho mining camps. The estimated value of the live stock owned in the county is $1,000,000. Union, the county seat, has a population of 800, and other thriving places are La Grande, Island City and Summerville.

WASCO COUNTY

lies mainly east of the Cascade Mountains. Population, 11,120. Area, over 4,000,000 acres. It is divided into districts by nature. The Dalles District has Dalles City, the county seat, for its centre, and includes the country watered by the streams that rise near Mount Hood, and empty into the Columbia or Des Chutes Rivers, reaching from the Cascade Mountains to the Des Chutes, and from the Columbia, on the north, to the Warm Spring Indian Reservation, on the south. Dalles City is situated upon and under a bluff, and is a place of much importance, containing 2,300 inhabitants. Back of the town are high hills, upon one of the highest of which is a farm of 500 acres, under good cultivation, thus demonstrating that the hill lands of Eastern Oregon can be made valuable in producing grain, hay, vegetables and fruit. As far back as the Tygh River, all the bottom-lands were settled twenty years ago, but lately the high plateaux are being taken up by immigrants. There are in this part of the country many wealthy stock-raisers. The uplands, bordered by the Columbia, and extending south for fifty miles, between the waters of the John Day and Des Chutes Rivers, and east to the boundary of Umatilla, form the John Day District. The soil is excellent, and it is a good grass section, the bunch-grass growing vigorously. The bottom-lands are very rich. The Blalock Ranch, the largest farm of the entire region, is situated at the junction of the Columbia and the John Day Rivers. It contains over 60,000 acres, and is under the control of enterprising men, who are trying coöperative farming on a great scale. The Middle District of Wasco County reaches from the Des Chutes River to the Blue Mountains. It is a well-watered section, and has thriving villages and trading points. The land is well adapted to agriculture, and, as soon as railroads reach this region, settlers will turn it into a rich farming district. The Ocheco District lies between the branches of the Crooked River, the south-eastern fork of the Des Chutes. Prinesville, the centre of trade, is a busy place, with several hundred inhabitants, supporting a newspaper, and doing a brisk trade with the mining districts in the south-western spurs of the Blue Mountains.

WASHINGTON COUNTY,

situated west of Multnomah, is one of the most attractive portions of the State, and was early settled. Population, 7,802. Area, 437,000 acres ; surveyed, 368,000 ; unsurveyed, 69,000 ; settled, 276,000. The face of the country is diversified. There are prairies broken by forests and streams, and skirted by hills on every side. Much care is given to horse-breeding and cattle-raising from pure-blooded stock. Hillsboro', the county seat ; Forest Grove, Beaverton, Gaston and Cornelius are the principal towns. The Pacific University, at Forest Grove, is a well-endowed and successful institution, and with it is connected a Government Indian school. The Oregon and California Railroad traverses a portion of the county.

YAMHILL COUNTY

lies west of Clackamas, and south of Washington. Population, 7,945. Area, 483,000 acres ; surveyed, 414,000 ; unsurveyed, 69,000 ; settled, 276,000. The land is for the most part prairie, although there are hilly ranges. The soil of the rolling uplands is excellent for wheat, and very large crops of the cereals, and of vegetables and fruit are produced. The county ranks third, with respect to the value of its farm products. Socially, it is second to none. There are many thriving towns and villages, among which may be named Amity, Sheridan, Dayton, Lafayette, North Yamhill and McMinnville. The Yamhill and Willamette Rivers are both navigable, and there are two railways in the county.

WASHINGTON TERRITORY.

CHEHALIS COUNTY

lies on the coast. It has an area of 2,800 square miles. Population, 921. Value of assessed property, $341,000 ; assessed acreage, 113,907. About one-third of the area is rich bottom land, and there are many beautiful prairie reaches. The Chehalis River Valley, which is the largest and most valuable agricultural region in Western Washington, varies in breadth from 15 to 50 miles. The soil produces very large crops of wheat, oats, barley, vegetables and fruit. The uplands are rough and timbered with cedar, fir, maple and ash. The pasture lands throughout the county are excellent, and make it eminently a place for dairying and stock-raising, as well as for farming. Butter produced is noted for quality and quantity. Game is plentiful in the mountains ; all the streams abound in fish. The rivers flowing into the ocean are frequented by salmon, and the various fisheries of the coast are richer than those of the Atlantic seaboard. Gray's Harbor, an important haven, lies in the county. In Chehalis County there is an immense quantity of Government and Northern Pacific Railroad land, of good quality, awaiting settlers, the line of the railroad passing along the entire eastern section. Montesano is the county seat, and other towns are Cedarville, Chehalis City and Satsop.

CLALLAM COUNTY

is also on the coast, its northern boundary being the Strait of Juan de Fuca. Its area is 2,050 square miles. Value of assessed property, $130,581 ; assessed acreage,

27,978. Population, 638. There is very good land along the strait, and the river bottoms have a rich soil. These latter, in their wild state, are covered with vine-maple, alder, and other deciduous growths, with groupings of hemlock, cedar and white fir. The ridges between the salt-water and foot-hills have much fir timber. There is excellent grazing, and all the cereals, vegetables, roots and fruits flourish. The climate is mild and equable. The woods abound in game, the rivers in fish, and the salt-water fisheries bid fair to develop into a profitable industry. The country is virtually unsettled, and offers no end of opportunity to those willing to reclaim the land. The principal towns are Port Angelos, New Dungeness and Neah Bay.

CLARKE COUNTY

is situated west of the Cascade Mountains, extending along the Columbia River a distance of 40 miles. Area, 725 square miles. Value of taxable property, $1,235,262; assessed acreage, 156,785. Population, 5,490. There is a great deal of level land, and but little that is too hilly for cultivation. Most of the country is heavily timbered, with open swales of from five to twenty-five acres, which may be easily cultivated and produce abundantly. There is a large quantity of Government land of this sort from ten to twenty miles from market, open to entry. The production are wheat, oats, barley, peas, vegetables and fruit, which yield finely. Cattle, horses, sheep and swine thrive on the good pasturage. Toward the mountains, where the hills are too steep for cultivation, settlers can use the Government lands for many years to come as stock ranges. There are several grist and saw mills in operation. Vancouver, the county seat, is the largest town. It is situated on the Columbia River, at the head of ocean navigation. There are thirty-nine school districts in which children are taught from three to ten months every year.

COLUMBIA COUNTY

lies in Eastern Washington. It has an area of 2,000 square miles. Value of taxable property, $2,454,383; assessed acreage, 102,622. Population, 7,103. The country is well-watered by the Touchet, Tucannon and Pataha Rivers. Timber is only to be found along the water-courses. The whole country is very fertile, wheat averaging thirty bushels per acre, and often yielding as much as fifty bushels. Sheep and wool-raising form an important industry. Dayton, the county seat, has a flourishing woolen mill, the product of which is over $50,000 annually, as well as planing mills, a sash and door factory, good schools, two newspapers and pleasant houses. Lumber is brought here from the Blue Mountains by means of a flume and supplied to the surrounding country. This town and Waitsburg, another thriving place on the Touchet River, are large trading centres, being distributors of the great wheat crops of the surrounding region, both being in connection with the Oregon Railway and Navigation Company's system. There are also several other prosperous towns in the county, among which may be named Pomeroy, with a flouring mill, Pataha and Marengo. Huntsville, another town, has a good educational establishment, under the charge of the United Brethren. It is estimated that there are at least 750,000 acres of good bunch-grass land in this county yet unsettled, nearly all of which is suitable for wheat-growing. This county has now been divided, and Garfield County formed of part of its territory.

COWLITZ COUNTY

is situated between Clarke and Wahkiakum Counties, the Columbia River being its southern boundary. Population, 2,062. Its area is 1,100 square miles. Value of assessed property, $816,000; assessed acreage, 174,497. The county is well-watered by many streams, and is traversed its entire length by the Cowlitz River, which is navigable during the entire year for thirty miles to Cowlitz Landing. The Northern Pacific Railroad also runs through it. The valley of the Cowlitz contains many fine farms, the soil being very rich. There are 26,000 acres under cultivation. The surface of the country is quite diversified, and forests of fir and cedar abound. There are, however, fine tracts of prairie still to be taken up, as only one-half of the county has been surveyed, and nearly one-third of the land is vacant. Numerous coal veins, still undeveloped, are known to exist. The exports are cattle, hogs, general farm and dairy produce, shingles and lumber. Kalama is the county seat. Freeport, on the Cowlitz, has a population of 300. At Oak Point there are a grist and saw-mill, and several salmon canneries along the Columbia River.

GARFIELD COUNTY

was organized in December, 1881, at which time Columbia County was partitioned and this county established. The description of Columbia County includes all that may be said of Garfield County at present.

ISLAND COUNTY

is composed of Whidby and Camano Islands, situated at the junction of Juan de Fuca and Rosario Straits and Admiralty Inlet. Area, 250 square miles. Value of taxable property, $349,547; assessed acreage, 98,490. Population, 1,087. Whidby Island has an area of 115,000 acres, of which the greater part is heavily timbered with fir and cedar. Camano Island comprises 30,000 acres, of which 28,000 are timber of the same varieties as those on Whidby. The arable lands of both islands produce good crops of wheat, hay, oats, barley, garden vegetables and fruit. Coupville is the county seat, and other villages are Coveland and Utsalada. At the latter place there is a large saw-mill.

JEFFERSON COUNTY

lies south of Clallam, on the coast, and has a large frontage on Hood's Canal. Area, 2,500 square miles. Value of taxable property, $569,128; assessed acreage, 87,191. Population, 1,712. There are several thriving farm settlements, but the chief industry is lumbering. Good iron ore has been found at Chimacum, near Port Townsend. This latter is the county seat, and also the port of entry for Puget Sound. The District Court is likewise held here, and the place is garrisoned by United States troops, and has the Marine Hospital among its establishments. At Port Ludlow and at Port Discovery are large steam saw-mills. Jefferson County offers a fair field for lumbering, dairying and farming, and but a tithe of its territory has been explored.

KING COUNTY

is situated on the eastern shore of Puget Sound. Area, 1,900 square miles. Value of taxable property, $2,454,706 ; assessed acreage 126,649   Population, 6,910. The face of the country is diversified by hill, valley, lake and stream. There are about 164,000 acres of agricultural land in the county. The remainder is heavily timbered with fir, spruce, hemlock, cedar and other trees. The cultivated lands produce large crops of vegetables, hay, hops, grain and fruit, and for mixed farming and dairying the country cannot be surpassed. There are extensive fields of excellent coal and large deposits of iron. Seattle, on Elliot Bay, is the county seat, with a population of nearly 4,000. This is an enterprising city, well built, delightfully situated, and doing an enormous business, principally in coal and lumber. It has a well sheltered harbor, entirely free from obstructions, with good anchorage, and water deep enough for the largest vessels alongside the wharves. The Territorial University, five school houses, many churches, two daily newspapers, several well-kept hotels, streets of substantial warehouses and stores, as well as beautiful residences on the heights overlooking the place, are some of the features of this busy city. It is connected with the coal fields at Newcastle by railroad, and it is the principal port on Puget Sound for the fleet of large passenger steamships in the Pacific coast trade and the steam colliers of the Oregon Improvement Company's lines. Besides the heavy exports of coal and lumber, there is a large business in salmon packing and in manufactures of wood, iron, flour, etc. The principal towns are Newcastle and Renton, in the coal region, Dwamish, White River, Snoqualmie and Slaughter. The havens are Salmon Bay, Seattle Bay and Quartermaster's Harbor, although safe anchorage may be found at almost any point.

KITSAP COUNTY

is a peninsula, with 80 miles of shore line on Admirality Inlet and 50 on Hood's Canal. It includes also Bainbridge and Blake's Islands. Area, 540 square miles. Value of taxable property, $933,848 ; assessed acreage, 54,891. Population, 1,738. Nearly all the surface of the county is heavily wooded, and six saw-mills of great capacity give employment to large numbers of men. Two of these mills and one grist-mill are situated at Port Gamble. The other saw-mills are at Seabeck, Port Madison and Port Blakely, and at all these places are flourishing settlements.

KLIKITAT COUNTY

is situated on the Columbia River, between Walla Walla and Skamania Counties on the east and west, and Yakima County on the north. Area, 2,088 square miles. Value of taxable property, $821,837 ; assessed acreage, 28,427. Population, 4,057. Of the million and a quarter acres included in the Government surveys, only about one-fourth has been entered, and the remainder, including numerous inviting valleys, awaits settlement. The Klikitat Valley is 20 miles wide and 30 long. Much good land is to be found in the county, and that which has been cultivated yields heavy crops of wheat. Klikitat is finely watered, and has always been a favorite stock-raising county on account of the abundant bunch-grass. The Simcoe

Mountains are covered with forests of fir, pine, and oak. Goldendale, the county-seat, has nearly 600 inhabitants and a good trade. Klikitat City and Columbus are also thriving places.

LEWIS COUNTY

is situated east of Pacific and north of Cowlitz and Clarke counties. Area, 1,800 square miles. Value of taxable property, $931,815; assessed acreage, 302,832. Population, 3,263. The county is well watered, has extensive undeveloped coal fields, and its surface is much diversified. There are ridge lands, heavily wooded with fir, cedar, maple and alder, and bottom lands covered with wild cherry, vine-maple and dogwood. Much of the land is already occupied, yet there is room for many new settlers. Wheat, barley and oats are prolific, and all garden vegetables yield large crops. The soil generally is a clayey loam. Chehalis is the county-seat. Other towns are Algernon, Boistfort, Cowlitz, Clequato, Little Falls and Winlock. The county is traversed by the Northern Pacific Railroad from north to south, and railroad lands are offered for sale.

MASON COUNTY

lies on the south-western shore of Puget Sound, south of Kitsap County. Area, 900 square miles. Value of taxable property, $226,565; assessed acreage, 61,607. Population, 559. Three-fourths of the county is rugged and mountainous, but the river valleys of the Skokomish and smaller streams, tributary to Hood's Canal, have good agricultural land. Stock-raising is the principal pursuit, there being excellent pasturage. Cereals and vegetables thrive, but hay is the chief product. The highlands are well covered with spruce, fir, hemlock, cedar and maple, and many persons are engaged in logging. Oakland is the county-seat. Other towns are Acadia, Skokomish and Union City.

PACIFIC COUNTY

is in the south-western part of the Territory, on the coast line. Area, 550 square miles. Value of taxable property, $334,000; assessed acreage, 53,096. Population, 1,654. The county is well watered by many streams, of which the Willopah and Nasul, emptying into Shoalwater Bay. are the largest, the latter being navigable for 50 miles by light-draught steamers. The bottom lands have deep, rich soil, are of an average width of ten miles, and are well adapted to agriculture. Vegetables grow to great size, and grain and fruit are produced largely on the cleared lands. Oysterville, the county-seat, is situated upon a sand peninsula, from one to three miles wide and twenty miles long, which forms the breakwater of Shoalwater Bay. Owing to lack of transportation facilities, the only exports are lumber, fish and oysters, the latter in large quantities. The lumber mills at Centreville and South Bend are busy establishments, the latter shipping 1,000,000 feet per month. A grist-mill is greatly needed, and one well managed would prove quite profitable. Other farms and settlements are Willopah, Bruceport, Ilwaco, a watering-place for the people of Portland, Chinoak and Pacific City. There are 21 school districts in which schools are open. Little more than half the land in the county is surveyed, and about one-quarter of that is still subject to entry.

PIERCE COUNTY

lies on the south-eastern shore of Puget Sound. Area, 1,800 square miles. Value of taxable property, $1,663,452 ; assessed acreage, 96,470. Population, 3,319. The valleys and plains of the Puyallup, Nisqually, and other streams are well adapted to mixed farming, dairying and stock-raising. Hop-growing is the principal occupation in the Puyallup Valley. The crop is very bountiful. There are extensive and rich deposits of semi-bituminous and lignite coal at Wilkeson, Carbonado and other places in the county, as well as quarries of building and limestone. There is much good timber, and at Old Tacoma there is a saw-mill with a capacity of 90,000 feet daily. The gravelly plain between Steilacoom and Mount Rainier is a beautiful natural park, but worthless for agricultural purposes. The lakes and streams abound in fish, and the woods in game of many kinds. Steilacoom is the county-seat. The principal town is New Tacoma, a port on the Sound, terminus of the Pacific division of the Northern Pacific Railroad, as well as the branch line to the coal mines at Wilkeson and Carbonado. This place is, next to Seattle, the busiest shipping point on Puget Sound. Other towns are Puyallup, Lake View, Wilkeson, Franklin, Nisqually and Sumner.

SAN JUAN COUNTY

is composed of the islands which form the Archipelago de Haro. These islands are San Juan, Waldron, Orcas, Shaw, Guemes, Lopez, Stewart, John's and Decatur. Area, 280 square miles. Value of taxable property, $181,167 ; assessed acreage, 11,495. Population, 948. The county-seat is on San Juan Island. There is a good proportion of agricultural and grazing land on most of the islands, although they are mainly mountainous. The inhabitants engage profitably in mixed farming, dairying and sheep-husbandry. The latter occupation prospers extraordinarily, as the animals find excellent pasture throughout the year on the wild mountain-grasses, and the wool clip is nearly three pounds per sheep. Vegetation is earlier than at the head of Puget Sound, and there is less rainfall than in other sections of West Washington Territory. There are valuable limestone deposits, and the lime kilns in operation turn out thousands of barrels of excellent lime. Silver ore has also recently been found. Much of the territory of these islands is unsettled. Game of all kinds, especially deer, is abundant

SKAMANIA COUNTY

is situated east of Clarke, and has the Columbia River for its southern boundary. Area, 2,800 square miles. Value of taxable property, $169,618 ; assessed acreage, 10,073. Population, 809. This county is traversed by the Cascade Mountains, and the limited area available for settlement along the Columbia has been for the most part taken up. Here are the great falls of the Columbia River, and through the mountain gorge the waters of this stream and its many tributaries force their way to the ocean. The principal occupation of the people is making cordwood from the fir with which the entire region is densely covered. Lower Cascades is the county-seat, and the other town is Upper Cascades.

SNOHOMISH COUNTY

is north of King County, and Admiralty Inlet is its western boundary. Area, 1,000 square miles. Value of taxable property, $368,667 ; assessed acreage, 86,232. Population, 1,387. There are vast tracts of marsh and tide-lands at the deltas of the Stillaquamish and Snohomish Rivers, much of which is cultivated, yielding heavy crops, especially of oats and barley. Hop-growing is also successful, and there is a great deal of good river-bottom land open to settlement. The country is densely wooded with fir, cedar and other forest trees, and lumbering is the principal industry. Snohomish City is the county-seat, and at Mukilteo is a large salmon-cannery. At Tulalip there is an Indian reservation. On the Skywhamish River are quartz and placer gold mines.

SPOKANE COUNTY

lies east and south of the Columbia River. Its area is very large, embracing all the great fertile plateaux which lie within the Big Bend of the Columbia River, and those known as the Spokane Plains in the northeast. Value of taxable property, $1,144,000 ; assessed acreage, 38,818. Population, 4,262. This county is traversed a distance of 108 miles by the Northern Pacific Railroad, on either side of which, in many places, there are great expanses of bunch-grass lands, with deep, rich soil inviting to cultivation. The country is well watered by lakes and streams, and much of it is admirably adapted to stock-raising on a large scale. Fertile wheat-producing lands are to be found in the Crab Creek region to the west, and in the Hangman, Pine and Rock Creek Valleys to the south and east of the railroad, as well as in many other localities. In the Cœur d'Alêne Mountains there are deposits of the precious and useful minerals, as well as most beautiful marble, as yet undeveloped. Spokane Falls, the county-seat, is a bustling, thriving town, with great natural advantages. It is destined to become a place of very great importance, owing to its situation on the main line of the Northern Pacific Railroad, its enormous water power, and the fact of its being at the head of the great cañon of the lower Spokane, which begins at the falls, and which is with difficulty crossed below. Through the medium of the Spokane River, Cœur d'Alêne Lake, and the streams which enter it, a great area of valuable timber land is tributary to the town by water. The town has already churches, public and private schools, newspapers, flouring and other mills, and is growing rapidly. Cheney, another flourishing town, situated on the railroad, is the seat of the District Court, and also of the land office of the Northern Pacific Railroad.

STEVENS COUNTY,

situated in the north-eastern part of the Territory, adjoining British Columbia, is one of the largest counties. Very little of its area has been surveyed, and it is quite sparsely settled, the population in 1880 being only 1,245. Value of taxable property, in 1881, $164,719 ; assessed acreage, 2,720. Its surface is that of a great rolling plateau, having many deep valleys, called coulées, the channels of former water-courses, with soil of the best sort for grain and grass. The country is well watered by countless streams, and is free from alkali. There are growths of good timber, consisting of spruce, white pine and large tamarack, throughout the region, interspersed with open arable land, which produces good crops of wheat and vegetables, as well as melons and tomatoes, wherever it has been tried. The climate is warmer than that of the Walla Walla Valley. Gold is found in the streams north of the Spokane River, and the mountainous region toward Lake Pend d'Oreille is rich in ledges of fine white and variegated marble, limestone and granite, as well as gold-bearing quartz. Horses in large droves are wintered in this county without care, subsisting on the bunch-grass. Colville is the county seat. At Kettle Falls (old Fort Colville) there is good salmon fishing, and game of all kinds is everywhere abundant.

THURSTON COUNTY

lies at the head of Puget Sound. Area, 750 square miles. Value of taxable property, $1,800,000; assessed acreage, 284,939. Population, 3,270. The surface of the county is densely wooded with fir, cedar, oak, ash, maple and alder. Logging is one of the chief industries. There is, however, much prairie and bottom land adapted to stock-raising and agriculture. The best butter is produced by the dairies of the county, and the cereals, garden vegetables and hardy fruits yield well. There is unlimited water at Tumwater, which is utilized by a saw-mill, water-pipe factory, two flouring-mills, a tannery, two door and sash factories, and the water-works, which supply the town of Olympia. This latter is a beautiful place of about 1,300 inhabitants. It is the county seat, as well as the capital of the Territory. Olympia is connected by a short railroad with Tenino, a station on the Northern Pacific Line.

WAKIAKUM COUNTY,

the smallest county in the Territory, is situated on the Columbia River, between Pacific and Cowlitz Counties. Area, 360 square miles. Value of taxable property, $259,728; assessed acreage, 22,000. Population, 1,600. The land is rocky and mountainous, abounding in dense growths of timber, and there is little agriculture carried on, excepting along the river, where garden vegetables and hay are produced. The people mainly engage in salmon-canning, and there are several large establishments for this purpose. Cathlamet is the county seat. Other towns are Waterford, Eagle Cliff and Skamokawa.

WALLA WALLA COUNTY

is bounded south and east by the Blue Mountains, and west and north by the Columbia and Snake Rivers. Area, 1,250 square miles. Value of taxable property, $4,421,000; assessed acreage, 134,861. Population, 8,716. The county is a high rolling prairie, well watered by many rivers and their lateral branches. About three-fourths of the land is arable, and experience has proved it to be extremely fertile, producing wheat, barley and oats to perfection. The average yield to the acre of the former is thirty bushels, and of the latter forty-five, although these figures are often exceeded. A peculiarity of the soil is that the crops grown on the top of the hills yield as heavily as those produced in the low-lands. Fruits of many varieties may be cultivated. Apples, peaches, cherries, pears, grapes, and different kinds of berries grow here of fine flavor and perfect in quality. This region, in addition to its enormous wheat yield, is well adapted, on account of its equable climate, to be the great fruit-producing area of the entire line of the Northern Pacific Railroad, and fruit will eventually form no small part of its products for export. Nearly all of the best lands in the county are taken up, and only improved farms may be purchased from owners who wish to sell out. Walla Walla, the county seat, finely situated on Mill Creek, a branch of the Walla Walla River, about eight miles from the base of the Blue Mountains, and containing

4,000 inhabitants, is a substantial city. There are many extensive business establishments, banks, fine public buildings, good schools, numerous churches, daily and weekly newspapers. The county is traversed by many miles of railroad of the Oregon Railway and Navigation Company's system, and is brought thereby into connection with the Northern Pacific Railroad.

WHATCOM COUNTY

is the north-eastern portion of Washington Territory, adjoining the British Possessions. Area, 3,840 square miles. Value of taxable property, $681,424; assessed acreage, 117,679. Population, 3,137. The county has half a million of acres of arable soil, consisting of tide bottom and uplands. The lands at the deltas of the Skagit, the Samish and the Nooksahk are extraordinarily rich, producing enormous harvests of oats, barley and hay, while potatoes and wheat yield heavily on the higher grounds. There is abundance of fir, cedar, spruce, maple and other timber, and water-power to convert it into lumber. There are large deposits of coal and potters' clay, quarries of excellent building stone, and gold placer mines are worked in the Skagit River. Fine opportunities are awaiting settlers at numerous points in the region. Whatcom is the county seat. Other towns are Schome and La Conner.

WHITMAN COUNTY

is situated east of the Columbia River and north of the Snake. Area, 4,300 square miles. Value of taxable property, $681,424; assessed acreage, 236,853. Population, 7,014. The surface of the county is rolling prairie-land, interspersed with many valleys and water-courses. The soil of the hills is a deep, rich loam, and of the valleys somewhat lighter. Toward the Palouse country it is deepest and richest. In some sections corn is raised, but wheat, oats and barley yield most richly. Flax is also cultivated and produces largely. Fruits also are prolific. There is a thick growth of bunch-grass covering the hills and valleys, and cattle, sheep and horses are raised in great numbers, the climate being mild enough to make stock-raising a profitable business. The horses are especially good, particularly draft-horses, bunch-grass being favorable to the development of muscle. There is but little timber in the county, that used being brought by flume from the Cœur d'Alêne Mountains in Idaho. Colfax is the county seat. The region is traversed to a great extent by the system of the Oregon Railway and Navigation Company's lines, and there are large tracts of fertile land open to immigrants.

YAKIMA COUNTY

lies west of the Columbia River, its northern boundary being the Wenatchee River and its southern Klikitat County. Area, 9,224 square miles. Value of taxable property, $1,019,349; assessed acreage, 403,072. Population, 2,811. In the county are a number of fertile valleys, among which are the Kittitas, 40 miles long and 15 wide; the Attaman, 25 miles long and 2 to 7 in width. The Yakima Indian Reservation is also a large fertile tract, more than 30 miles long, which, if put under cultivation, would produce largely. Stock-raising is the principal occupation, and large herds and flocks roam over the country. Wheat yields large harvests, having averaged 30 bushels to the acre in 1881, and oats and barley from 40 to 50.

Tomatoes, corn, melons, grapes and peaches have also been grown successfully. There are 480,000 acres awaiting settlement. In the Cascade Mountains placer and quartz gold mining are carried on to some extent, and deposits of cinnabar and antimony exist. Yakima City, the county seat, has a population of about 300 inhabitants, with two churches, a good school, a district court and a hotel.

SUGGESTIONS TO EMIGRANTS.

Good health is the first requisite of a person who proposes to emigrate to a new country, with a view to improving his condition in life. Although the climate of the Pacific North-west is so favorable as to insure exemption from many diseases which prevail in other States, and to promise relief in certain ailments, the chances are that immigration will prove a mistake in the case of invalids who are compelled to work for a living. Buoyancy of spirit, enabling one to bear up under disappointment and hardships, which, as a rule, only characterizes a sound body, is nowhere more needed than in a strange land among strangers.

Persons beyond the active years of life, and without that adaptability to circumstances belonging to them, will also run considerable risk in emigrating, unless possessed of means. To such, old communities usually afford better opportunities for self-support than new ones, where the struggle for success in life calls for more energy than pertains to mature age. Single men are obviously much safer in taking their chances than persons who have to provide for others. Heads of families, especially, even if strong in body and not too advanced in life, should carefully weigh the possible consequences of emigration, both to themselves and to those whose future will be fashioned by their own.

No one should think of emigrating without sufficient means for self-support for at least a short time after reaching his destination ; for suitable employment immediately after arrival cannot always be relied on, and there is nothing more discouraging to the new-comer than to become a subject of public or private charity. This caution applies particularly to heads of families, who would be cruelly derelict in their duty to expose those depending on them to the risk of destitution on arrival. Families who contemplate settling on lands will require, after providing for all traveling expenses, about five hundred dollars with which to meet the cost of putting up a house, for live-stock, seed, farming utensils, provisions, etc.

Success can be promised to energetic farmers. However modest their beginning, they may be sure of finding themselves in possession of a competency after a few laborious years. But there is not only a fine opening for small farmers; nowhere else will stock-raising and ordinary farming on a large scale bring more satisfactory results. Many farmers who are now rich, at first rented farms on shares, and so earned money to buy them. Good men, who wish to begin in this way, have no difficulty in finding farms to rent, especially west of the Cascade Mountains. Good practical farmers, with slender means, might do well to try this plan for a year or two. By renting a farm, the new comer can gain all necessary information about the country before settling permanently. He will thus avoid the mistakes which often happen from locating in haste. The usual rates of rent are one-half the crop to the owner if he supplies seed, team, etc., and one-third the crop if only the land and the permanent improvements thereon are furnished. The cost of wheat-farming in average years will not exceed $7.50 per acre for the ploughing, harrowing, seeding, harvesting, hauling and threshing. The interest on the value of the land might be placed at $2.50. This would give a total of $10 an acre at a liberal estimate for all labor expended and cost incurred.

Land in all stages of improvement and grades of cultivation may be purchased in the Willamette Valley, and at almost every other point. Twelve years ago, improved farms could be bought readily for $15 to $20 per acre, and the distant brush or oak grub lands at from $3 to $4. With the advent of the railroads, these prices gradually advanced, until now the best farms, held in tracts of 160 to 320 acres, sell at the firm price of $30 to $40 per acre. Near Salem and Albany the prices range from $50 to $60. Brush and light oak lands cannot now be obtained in advantageous situations for less than $12 to $15 per acre. Hill cleared lands which, in 1872, were regarded as fit for pasture only, and sold for $10 per acre, now command $20 and $25, dependent on location and county. There are, however, numbers of farms, less desirably situated as to lines of transportation, which may be bought at far lower rates. Take the average farming land of this class in the Willamette Valley, and prices, perhaps, will range from $15 to $35.

The immigrant who has some money will always do better here, as everywhere else, by investing in land already under cultivation than by purchasing wild lands, provided he is careful not to pay too high a price and to secure a good title. A small farm, well tilled, will afford a good living at once, obviating the loss of time and the hardship incident to a new settlement. The greater number of settlers, however, are not in the position to adopt the more advantageous course, and must avail themselves of the many openings for settlement on government or railroad lands. To them the fact is of great importance that the mild climate greatly mitigates the discomforts of the first few years, and that the legitimate rewards of the husbandman's toil are nowhere more certain to be reaped.

Generally speaking, persons accustomed to ordinary and mechanical labor, and who unite frugal habits with persevering industry, will run the least risk in emigrating; but individuals unwilling to work, or accustomed to live by their wits, are not wanted. Idlers will only go from bad to worse; and adventurers will not prosper.

Farm labor is worth from $25 to $30 per month and board. During winter some days will be lost. Harvest work is worth $1.50 per day. Good choppers are in demand, and on Puget Sound the lumber mills pay as high as $60 to $90 per month for first-class hands. A good worker can always find employment. Chinamen work for the railroads and board themselves at $1 per day, and in winter take contracts for grubbing brush land. New comers can find work with the railroads, which pay as follows: Common laborers, $1.75 to $2 a day; foremen of gangs from $75 to $100 a month; blacksmiths, $2.50 to $4 a day; carpenters, $3.50, and carpenter's assistants, $1.75 to $2; track layers (iron men), $2 to $2.50; men with their own teams, $4.50; assistant engineers (on construction), $125 to $150 per month and expenses. In railroad shops machinists get $3.50 to $4 per day; boiler makers, $4; helpers, $2.50 to $3; blacksmiths, $3 to $4; their helpers, $2.50 to $3; carpenters, $3.50; car repairers, $2 to $2.50;

painters, $3.50 ; laborers, $2 to $2.50; track layers, $1.85 to $2 per day. Harness makers, in Portland, $2 to $4 a day ; saddle makers get $3 to $5 a day for piece work. Cabinet making is extensively carried on. Good workmen receive steady employment and get $2.25 to $2.50 per day ; carpenters average $2.50 to $3 a day. The Portland wagon and carriage makers earn $2.50 to $3 ; blacksmiths on wagon and carriage work, $2.50 to $4 a day ; bricklayers and stonemasons, $4 a day. The woolen mills at Oregon City pay as follows : Common labor, $1.25 to $1.50; Chinese, 90c. to $1 ; weavers average $1.75 ; spinners, $1.25 to $1.50, being generally expert children and youths. House servants are in demand, and, owing to the absence of white help, Chinese are freely employed at $3 to $5 a week, very good ones earning as much as $25 to $30 a month. Servant girls earn good wages, and are preferred when they can be had.

There is not more lack here than in other parts of the United States of lawyers, doctors and clergymen. Persons belonging to these professions will find it difficult to make their way. But, even in these callings, success may be achieved by capable men.

In mercantile pursuits the opening is good for men of enterprise and capital ; but the chances for mere clerks are not the best.

WHEN AND HOW TO REACH THE COUNTRY.

Spring is the best season for immigration; next, summer ; then autumn, and winter the worst. In spring, the chances of finding employment are better than at any other time of the year, and those who take up land, or rent or purchase farms, can go at once to work.

At present, Portland is the most convenient point for emigrants. This city is the gateway and distributing point of the whole country, and from it all transportation routes diverge. Go to Portland, and thence to final destination.

Emigrants from Europe may reach Portland either by way of New York and thence by Pacific Mail Steamship Company's line to Panama, or by rail overland ; or else they may go direct by English or German steamers to the Isthmus, taking the regular steamers thence to San Francisco and Portland. Emigrants from Eastern Canada and the Atlantic States may either take the Panama route or go by rail across the continent to San Francisco and thence to Portland by the Oregon Railway and Navigation Company's steamships. The time from New York via Panama is about thirty days, and by the overland railroads the journey is made : first-class, in ten days, and by emigrant train in fifteen days.

By the Panama route, cooked food and sleeping accommodations are furnished, without extra charge ; by the overland route, the fare charged pays for transportation only, as far as San Francisco, while on the steamers from San Francisco to Portland, food and berths are included. For emigrants from the Middle and Western States, the overland route is unquestionably the best.

Though it is not practicable to charter cars for colonies, the use of a special car, westward, from Omaha, or Kansas City, can be obtained, when the number of passengers is sufficient.

Sleeping-car rates, first-class, overland, are as follows :

	Berths.	Sections.
New York to Chicago or St. Louis	$5 00	$10 00
Chicago or St. Louis to Omaha	3 00	6 00
Omaha to Ogden	5 00	10 00
Ogden to San Francisco	6 00	12 00

From Ogden to San Francisco the Central Pacific Railroad Company has now third-class sleeping-cars, fitted with upper and lower berths. These cars are a great convenience. Heretofore emigrants have been compelled to sit up, or make shift to rest as best they could. No additional charge is made for berths in third-class sleeping-cars. One hundred pounds free baggage is allowed for each whole ticket, and 50 pounds for each half ticket, between Eastern points and San Francisco. Excess of this rate costs $10 per 100 pounds from Omaha to San Francisco. From San Francisco to Portland, the Oregon Railway and Navigation Company allow free 150 pounds of baggage with each adult passenger; half-fare passengers in proportion. All baggage above this weight is charged for at the rate of two cents per pound.

The Oregon Railway and Navigation Company's steamships, between Portland and San Francisco, leave each port every few days. These steamships are large new vessels, which rank among the finest afloat. They are fitted up with every convenience and luxury known to modern travel. The trip between San Francisco and Portland is made in about two days, and affords the traveler full opportunity to enjoy the great scenic beauty of the Lower Columbia River.

There is another route to Oregon, overland, via Sacramento and Redding, which involves change of cars at Sacramento and includes 285 miles of staging, over high mountains, and still another change to cars at Roseburg, a point 200 miles south of Portland. This is frequently traveled in the summer by tourists, but involves much greater expense than emigrants are often willing to incur.

Passengers who go overland will in every case save money by purchasing through tickets, which may be obtained at the offices of all the great railroad lines. The fares to Portland from Atlantic seaboard and interior cities are constantly changing. At present, the rates for emigrants tickets, via San Francisco, and Oregon Railway and Navigation Company, are as follows :

Austin, Texas, $87.50 ; Atchison, Kan., $57.50 ; Bay City, Mich., $76.60 : Baltimore, Md., $73 ; Boston, Mass., $78.50 ; Buffalo, N. Y., $79 ; Burlington, Ia., $64.25 ; Cedar Rapids, Ia., $63.60 ; Chariton, Ia., $60.35 ; Chattanooga, Tenn., $80.50 ; Cheyenne, Wyo., $53 ; Clinton, Ia., $64 60 ; Cincinnati, O., $69.50 ; Cleveland, O., $76 ; Columbus, O., $73.10 ; Chicago, Ill., $68 ; Dallas, Tex., $79.30 ; Davenport, Ia., $63.45 ; Decatur, Ill., $67 ; Denison, Tex., $77 ; Denver, Col., $55 ; Des Moines, Ia., $59.76 ; Detroit, Mich., $74 ; Erie, Pa., $77.50 ; Evansville, Ill., $69.50 ; Florence, Kan., $57 50 ; Fort Wayne, Ind., $72.45 ; Galveston, Tex., $89.45 ; Grand Junction, Ia., $59.30 ; Grand Rapids, Mich., $73.45 ; Great Bend, Kan., $57.50 ; Green Bay, Wis., $73.90 ; Hannibal, Mo., $63.15 ; Harrisburg, Pa., $81.75 ; Houston, Tex., $87.95 : Indianapolis, Ind., $70 ; Iowa City, Ia., $63.39 ; Jackson, Mich., $74 ; Jefferson City, Mo., $62.25 : Jonesville, Mich., $73.15 ; Kansas City, Mo., $57.50 ; Kalamazoo, Mich., $72.25 ; Kearney Junction, Neb., $55 ; Keokuk, Ia., $64.25 ; Lafayette, Ind., $69.50 ; Lawrence, Kan., $57.50 ; Las Vegas, N. M., $55 ; Leavenworth, Kan., $57.50 ; Logansport, Ind., $70.50 ; Louisville, Ky., $69.50 ; Madison, Wis., $70.75 ; Mansfield, O., $75.85 ; Memphis, Tenn., $78.25 ; Milwaukee, Wis., $70.50 ; Minneapolis, Minn., $69.05 ; Moberly, Mo., $61.55 ; Montgomery, Ala., $81 ; Montreal, Can., $82 ; Nashville, Tenn., $74.50; Newark, O., $73 ; New Orleans, La., $78 ; New York, N. Y., $69.50 ; Niagara Falls, N. Y., $79 ; Omaha, Neb., $55 ; Oshkosh, Wis., $71.95 ; Peoria, Ill.. $65.25 ; Philadelphia, Pa., $69 ; Pittsburgh, Pa , $78.50 ; Portland, Me., $85.75 ; Pueblo, Col., $55 ; Quebec, Can., $83 ; Quincy, Ill., $64.40 ; Russell, Kan., $57.50 ; St. Joseph, Mo., $57.50 ; St. Louis, Mo., $66 ; St. Paul, Minn., $69.05 ; St. Thomas, Can., $77.40 ; Sedalia, Mo., $60.35 ; Topeka, Kan., $57.50 ; Vinita, Ind. Ter., $65.90.

Parties going to Oregon by way of Chicago will find at the office of the Oregon Railway and Navigation Company, No. 52 Clark street, full information with respect to routes and connections, and locations in Oregon and Washington will be freely described and pamphlets furnished. Upon arriving at Portland immigrants will find it to their advantage to call at the office of the Oregon Railway and Navigation Company, corner Front and D streets, where valuable information can be obtained.

But one class of tickets (first-class) is sold over river lines Emigrants' movables are carried at greatly reduced rates. The steamers and trains of the Oregon Railway and Navigation Company leave Portland daily for The Dalles, Walla Walla, Eastern Oregon and all Columbia and Snake River points, and steamers also connect daily at Kalama with the Northern Pacific Railroad for Tacoma, Seattle and Victoria. Trains also leave Portland daily on the Oregon and California railroad lines for all points in the Willamette Valley.

RULING PRICES.

Taken in the aggregate, the cost of living is less in Oregon and Washington Territory than in the Atlantic States, and no greater than in the Western States. Some commodities and general merchandise are held at higher prices than east of the Rocky Mountains; but all the products of the soil are comparatively cheap, notwithstanding the higher rates of wages. For the past two years, wheat in bulk at Portland has ranged from 80 cents to $1.60 per cental ; oats, 45 to 50 cents ; potatoes, 40 to 75 cents ; flax seed, $2, and onions, $1 per bushel ; best quality flour, $4.50 to $5 per barrel. Good farm horses cost about $100 each ; oxen, $125 per yoke ; good average milch cows, $25 ; sheep, $1.25 to $2.50 per head ; wool, common graded, 25 cents per pound ; beef on the hoof is worth 3 to 4 cents ; butchered beef, 5 to $7\frac{1}{2}$ cents ; choice cuts, 10 to 14 cents ; chickens, per dozen, $3 to $5 ; tame ducks, per pair, $1.50 ; geese, per pair, $3 ; turkeys, per pair, $3; wild ducks, per pair, 50 to 75 cents ; wild geese, per pair, $1.50 ; pheasants, per pair, 62 cents ; grouse, per pair, 75 cents ; venison, 10 to 12 cents per pound. Subjoined is the list of prices which ruled at Portland in December, 1881, for the articles named :

AGRICULTURAL IMPLEMENTS.

Farm wagons, $103 to $140.
Gang plough, $100 to $110.
Walking plow, $10 to $30.
Buckeye grain-drill, nine to eighteen hoe, $110 to $140.
Buckeye seeder and cultivator, eleven to fourteen tooth, $90.
Fan mills, $35 to $40.
Feed mills (choppers), $65 to $100.
Spring wagons, $140 to $260.

COFFEE.

Old Government Java, per pound, 20 to 22 cents.
Costa Rica, per pound, 15 to 15½ cents.
Guatemala, 13½ to 14½ cents.

COAL OIL.

Crystalline, 30 cents.
Downer's, 40 cents.
Standard brands, per gallon, 30 to 35 cents.
Leval oil, 110 degrees, 30 cents.

CANDLES.

Paraffine, per pound, 22½ to 25 cents.
Grant's, per pound, 13½ cents.
Gross & Co., per pound, 15 cents.
Emery's, 12 cents.

DAIRY PRODUCTS.

Butter, fancy, fresh roll, per pound, 32½ cents; good to fair, 15 to 30 cents; common, all shapes, 10 to 20 cents.
Oregon cheese, new factory, per pound, 14 to 16 cents; good to choice, 15 to 16 cents.
Eggs, per dozen, 35 cents.

DRIED FRUITS.

Apples, machine cured, per pound, 10 cents.
Apples, sun cured, per pound, 7 cents.
Pears, sun cured, per pound, 5 to 6 cents.
Pears, machine cured, box, 10 cents.
Peaches, Plummer dried, per pound, 12 to 14 cents.
Plums, sun cured, pitless, per pound, 10 cents.
Plums, machine cured, box, 15 to 18 cents.
Figs, California, twenty-five pound boxes, 7 to 8 cents.

DRY GOODS.

Standard sheeting, 4-4, 7½ to 8½ cents.
Light sheeting, 4-4, 5 to 7 cents.
Fine brown shirting, ¾, 7½ to 9½ cents.
Fine brown shirting, 4-4, 9 to 10 cents.
Brown drilling, 9½ to 10½.
Bleached shirting, ¾, 6½ to 8½ cents.
Bleached shirting, ⅞, 7½ to 9½ cents.
Bleached sheeting, 6-4, 15 to 21 cents.
Bleached sheeting, 8-4, 19 to 24 cents.
Bleached sheeting, 9-4, 21 to 26 cents.
Hickory stripes, 12½ cents.
Cheviot stripes, 10 to 15 cents.
Denims, brown and blue, 10 to 20 cents.
Checks, blue and brown, 12½ to 17½ cents.
Canton flannel, 9 to 20 cents.
Ticks, light, ⅞, 10 to 12 cents.
Ticks, heavy, ⅞, 15 to 23 cents.
Duck, white, 27 inches, 12½ cents.
Duck, white, 40 inches, 18 cents.
Duck, brown and blue, 18 cents.
Kentucky jeans, 18 to 37 cents.
Glazed cambric, 6 cents.
Prints: Spragues, per yard, 6 cents; Durnell, Cocheco, American, Hamilton, Richmond, Simson's, Corner, Pacific, Oriental, Allen's, per yard, 7 to 8 cents. Second quality, 5½ cents.
Fine family E blankets, $8.50 to $9.50.
Fine family F blankets, $6 to $9.50.
54 x 66 inch crib blankets, $3.75 to $4.

FLOUR, FEED, ETC.

Flour, fancy extra, per barrel, $5; country brands, $4 to $4.75.
Corn meal, per one hundred pounds, $2.75.
Buckwheat, per one hundred pounds, $4.50 to $5.
Oatmeal, per one hundred pounds, $4.25 to $4.50.
Cracked wheat, per one hundred pounds, $3.50.
Bran, per ton, $14.
Shorts, per ton, $22 50.
Middlings, per ton, fine, $22 to $25.
Hay, per ton, $14.

GRAIN.

Wheat, good to choice, per one hundred pounds, $1.60; fair to good, $1.55; Walla Walla, good to choice $1.95 to $1.97½; Walla Walla, fair to good, $1.90 to $1.95.
Oats, per one hundred pounds, choice milling, $1.40; good feed, $1.25; ordinary feed, $1.15.
Barley, per one hundred pounds, brewing, $1.35 to $1.40.
Rye, per one hundred pounds, nominal, $1.50 to $2.

HONEY.

Honey in comb, per pound, 16 cents; strained, in 5-gallon tins, per pound, 12½ cents; 1-gallon tins, per dozen, $14.50; ½-gallon tins, per dozen, $7 to $7.50; 5-gallon tins, 12 cents per pound.

HIDES, WOOL AND BAGS.

Hides, dry, over 16 pounds, per pound, 17½ to 18 cents.
Murrain hides, wet, 16 pounds, 14 cents.
Hides, wet salted, over 55 pounds, per pound, 8 cents.
Pelts, long wool, per skin, 30 cents; medium to short, 15 cents.
Shearlings, 5 to 8 cents.
Deer-skins, per pound, 19 to 22½ cents.

Beaver-skins, per pound, $1.60 to $1.75.

Wool, Eastern Oregon, per pound, 19 to 22 cents; Valley, 24 to 26 cents; Umpqua, 25 to 27 cents.

Grain-sacks, hand-sewed, 22 x 36, 9 to 10 cents.

Wool-sacks, 50 cents.

Gunnies, 14 cents.

GROCERIES.

Curry powder and paste, cases of three dozen, $5.

Salad oil, cases of one dozen quarts, $9; two dozen pints, $5; and four dozen and one-half pints, $3 per dozen.

Tapioca, sago, per pound, 7½ cents.

Fine table salt in jars, $1.75; papers, per dozen, 75 cents.

Best cider vinegar in casks, per gallon, 30 cents.

Pilot bread, fresh from bakeries, 4 cents per pound; soda crackers, 6 cents; butter, sugar and other crackers at same rates.

GREEN FRUITS.

Apples, per fifty-pound box, choicest, 60 to 80 cents.

Oranges, per one hundred, Los Angeles, $2 to $4.

Lemons, per one hundred, Los Angeles, $3.

Limes, per one hundred, California, $2.50.

Pears. per box, 50 to 75 cents.

Plums, per box, $1.25.

Cranberries, per barrel, Eastern, $15.

HARDWARE, ETC.

Axes, $10 to $14 per doz.

Axes, handled add., $12.50 to $16.50.

Augers, Douglass extra, discount 30 per cent.

Axles, iron, per pound, 8 cents.

Anvils, Wright, per pound, 13¼ cents.

Bits, Auger, Douglass, discount 25 per cent. New list.

Bells, cows, discount 50 per cent.

Brushes, horse, per dozen, $6 to $16.

Butts, cast, fast, discount 45 per cent.

Butts, cast, loose, discount 40 per cent.

Bolts, carriage, R B & W, discount 45 per cent.

Cartridges, Henry rifle, $10.40.

Chisels, extra frame and firmer, discount 50 per cent.

Coil chain, per pound, 7 to 9 cents.

Portland horse nails, No. 7, 25 cents; No. 8, 24 cents; No. 9, 43 cents per pound.

Grindstones. Berea, 2¼ cents.

Handles, axe, No. 1, per dozen, $3.25.

Handles, pick, No. 1. $3.

Hatchet's, Blood's list, 5 to 10 per cent. discount.

Hinges, strap, light, 40 per cent. discount.

Hinges, strap, heavy, 40 per cent. discount.

Round iron, ¾ to 2-inch, per pound, 4 cents.

Norway, 7 cents.

Horse-shoes, per keg, $5.75.

Horse-shoe shapes, per pound, 7 cents

Lead, bar, per pound, 7½ cents.

Locks, R & E, list Jan. 1.

Mattocks, $13 to $16.50.

Nails, ten to sixty, $4.50.

Nails, eightpenny, $4.75.

Nails, sixpenny, $5.

Nails, fourpenny, $5.25.

Oil-tempered springs, per pound, 14 cents.

Powder, agents' rates.

Planes, Greenfield Tool Co., list 20 per cent. off.

Rope, Oregon, 12½ cents.

Rope, California, 15 cents.

Saws, Disston, hand and panel, list 10 off.

Saws, S and Jackson, hand 26-inch, per dozen, $18.

Saws, x-cut, per foot, 40 cents.

Spikes, $4.75.

Shot, $2.10.

Shovels, L H Rd point, light, $8.50 to $13.50.

Shovels, L H Rd point, Ames, $13.50.

Steel plough tire, steel spring, 8 cents.

Steel, cast, 15½ cents.

Scales, Fairbanks, 10 per cent. off list.

Screws, gimlet-point, discount 20 per cent. off.

Traps, Newhouse, discount 15 per cent. from list.

Vises, solid box, Wright, 16 cents.

Wrenches, Coe's genuine, discount 40 per cent. off.

Wringers, clothes, per dozen, $55 to $65.

POTATOES AND VEGETABLES.

Potatoes, per one hundred pounds, 50 to 75 cents.

Cabbage, per pound, ¾ cents.

Turnips, per pound, 1 cent.

Carrots, per pound, 1 cent.

Beets, per pound, 1¼ cents.

Sweet potatoes, per pound, 1¼ to 1½ cents.

Onions, red, per pound, 1¼ cents.

PEASE, SEEDS, ETC.

Beans, per pound, Pea, 4½ cents; S. W., 4½; Bayou, 2½; Limas, 6 cents.

Pease, field, 2 cents; sweet, $3.

Timothy seed, 6 to 10 cents.

Red clover, 16 to 18 cents.

White clover, 35 cents.

Alfalfa, 8 to 10 cents.

Hungarian grass, 8 cents.

POULTRY.

Chickens, per dozen, large, $3 to $5.

Geese, per dozen, nominal, $6 to $9.

Turkeys, per pound, 18 to 20 cents.

Ducks, per dozen, wild, $4 to $4.50.

RICE.

Japan, table, per pound, 6 cents.

China, per pound, 5 to 6 cents.

SALT.

Liverpool (fine), large sacks, $16 to $20 per ton.
Liverpool (fine), factory filled, fifty-pound sacks, $20 to $25.
Liverpool (coarse), large sacks, $16 to $20.
Carmen Island, per ton, $10 to $12.
Ground rock (stock), per ton, $10 to $11.

TEAS.

Japan, Oolong, Young Hyson (papers), per pound, 30 to 40 cents.
Japan, Oolong and Young Hyson (lacquered boxes), per pound, 40 to 60 cents.
English breakfast, per pound, 60 to 75 cents.
Imperial gunpowder, per pound, 60 to 75 cents.
Common teas, per pound, 25 to 30 cents.

SUGARS.

Crushed sugar, barrels, 13¼ cents per pound; ½ barrels, 13½ cents per pound.
Powdered sugar, barrels, 13½ cents per pound; ½ barrels, 13¾ cents per pound.
Brown sugar, S. F. Refined Gold, 6, barrels, 11¾ cents per pound; Gold C. ½ barrels, 12 cents per pound.
Dry granulated, 12¾ cents per pound; Sandwich Island sugar, 8 to 11 cents per pound.

SMOKED MEATS.

Hams, Oregon cured, 15 to 16 cents per pound; Eastern cured, 18 to 19 cents per pound; California cured, 16 to 17 cents per pound.
Bacon, sides, 15 to 15½ cents per pound; breakfast, 15 to 15½ cents per pound; bacon, shoulders, 10 to 11 cents per pound.

CANNED GOODS.

Tomatoes, per dozen, 2½ pounds each, $1.25 to $1.50.

Corn, per dozen, 2 pounds each, $2 to $2.25.
Pease, per dozen, 2 pounds each, $2 to $2.15.
String Beans, per dozen, 2 pounds each, $1.75 to $2.
Peaches, per dozen, 2½ pounds each, $2.50 to $3.

SYRUPS.

California Refineries, in kegs, 75 cents per gallon.
California Refineries, in barrels, 70 cents per gallon.
California Refineries, in 1-gallon cans, 82 cents per gallon.

PAINT MATERIALS AND OILS.

White lead, best quality, in kegs, 8½ to 9 cents per pound.
Linseed oil, boiled, pure, per gallon, 72 cents.
Linseed oil, raw, pure, per gallon, 70 cents.
Litharge, per pound, 9 cents.
Prince's metallic paint, per pound, 2¼ cents.
Yellow Ochre, per pound, 3 cents.
Whiting, English, per pound, 3 cents.
Paris White, per pound, 3 to 3½ cents.
Lampblack, Eddy's, per pound, 35 to 40 cents.
Turpentine, per gallon, 80 cents.
Lard oil, standard brands, pure, in barrels, $1.10 to $1.15 per gallon; in cans, $1.15 to $1.20 per gallon.
Lard oil, No. 1, barrels, $1.00 to $1.05 per gallon.
Lard oil, No. 1, cases, $1.05 to $1.10.
Dogfish oil, refined, in cases, per gallon, 60 cents.
Dogfish oil, common, in cases, per gallon, 47½ cents.
Salmon oil, in cases, per gallon, 40 cents.
Sperm oil, in cases, $1.00.
Mineral Sperm, in cases, per gallon, 52½ to 55 cents.

TEMPERATURE AND RAINFALL.

Statement showing the Maximum and Minimum Temperatures, the Mean Temperature and Rainfall, in inches and hundredths, at the places named, for the years 1879, 1880, and 1881 to date; also the Annual Mean Temperature and Total Rainfall for the same years. Compiled from the Records on file at the Office of the Chief Signal Officer, U. S. Army, Washington, D. C.

PORTLAND, OREGON.

Latitude, 45° 30′ *N. Longitude west from Greenwich,* 122° 27′ 36″. *Elevation of Barometer above sea level,* 66.50 *feet.*

MONTH.	1879.				1880.				1881.			
	Temperature.			Rainfall.	Temperature.			Rainfall.	Temperature.			Rainfall.
	Max.	Min.	Mean.		Max.	Min.	Mean.		Max.	Min.	Mean.	
January........	52	20	37.8	5.28	57	26.5	41.9	12.27	57	21	39	8.57
February........	60	25	44.0	13.22	52	26.5	38.1	5.67	63	26	45.5	13.36
March............	73 5	33	48.8	11.70	58	25.5	41.4	4.48	31	49.2	2.33
April.............	77	35.5	52.3	2.19	85	33	50.3	2.92	79.5	40	55.1	3.51
May.............	81.7	41	54.6	6.60	76	55	53.9	8.13	81.9	39.9	58.1	1 38
June............	81.7	43.5	60.5	2.18	89.5	42	60.4	1.59	85.4	45.4	60.8	2.34
July	91.7	47.5	66.1	1.75	92	46	66.1	.59	90.5	46.3	68.4	1.16
August...........	86.7	50	68.0	.97	87.5	46.5	63.8	1.31	85.7	46.1	65.4	2.11
September	85.3	43.7	63.7	2.18	79.5	41.5	59.8	1.34	80 8	40.4	60.6	2.64
October.........	67.5	37 2	51.9	4 23	74	34	52.7	1.47	63.8	32.0	47.1	6 60
November	61.3	25.3	43.6	4.56	64	2.25	42.2	3.17	58.0	29.0	43.0	6.91
December..	58	3.0	38.9	7.36	63	19	39.7	13.93	58.2	29.2	43.2	6.67

Total rainfall .... 62.22 .... 51.87 .... 58.08

OLYMPIA, WASHINGTON TERRITORY.

January.	48	19	36.2	5.96	50	11	36.6	19.69	53	23	38.8	8.90
February........	54	24	40 2	15 59	49	25	36.7	5.16	58	24	43.8	16.28
March...........	65	29	44.8	14.44	58	23	39.7	5.57	71	29	46.6	4.03
April...........	69	32	48.6	2.10	82	28	46.9	2.47	74	32	50 9	4.93
May.	76	35	52.4	4.72	75	33.5	50.7	4.10	78	33	53.0	1.54
June...	76	38	57.8	.41	88	36	57.9	1.41	83	40	58.0	1.93
July	83.5	41	60.7	2.62	93.5	42	62.3	.52	87	41	59.6	0 98
August...........	85	42	62.7	2.11	83	41	60.8	22	84	42	59.8	0 71
September......	81	39	57.0	2.88	73	34	54.5	1.05	78	39	55.8	2.47
October.........	62	27	47.9	6.17	73		49 3	2.83	61	22	47.4	8.18
November	59	26	42.0	5.49	58	23	39.2	3 06	57	32	43.6	6.75
December.... ..	56	8	37.6	11.42	59	20	39.8	16.66	..	.....	.....	.....

Total rainfall.................78.44.....................62.77 Eleven mos......56.70

DAYTON, WASHINGTON TERRITORY.

Observations commenced Dec. 1, 1879.

January.........	......	......	......	...	......	61	13	*	3 37	47	2	*	5.03
February.........	......	......	......		.....	54	8	......	2.19	64	6	......	5.04
March	......	......	......	...	.....	75	8	......	1.89	43	25	......	1.81
April............	......	......	......	...	.....	91	21	......	3.81	83	28	......	3.51
May.............	......	......	......	.. ...	......	90	31	... ...	2.78	85.6	30	... .	.45
June...........	......	......	......	...	......	97	39	... ...	1.00	86.9	26.5	......	1 61
July	......	......	......	...	......	102	42	... ..	1.68	90.0	37.4	......	.65
August.	......	......	......	...	......	93	42	.. ...	1.29	96 0	38.4	......	.22
September......	......	......	......	...	......	88	34	......	.19	91.3	29 0	.....	1.47
October.........	......	......	......	...	......	92	27	......	1.65	71.0	19.0	.....	3.04
November	.. ...	......	......	...	......	63	8	......	3 00	57 0	5.0	.....	2.47
December........	54	17	......	4.55	55	0	......	7.93	......	......	......	......

Total rainfall...................29.78 Eleven mos..... 25.33

* No observations of mean temperature deduced.

LEWISTON, IDAHO.

Observations commenced Nov. 23, 1879.

MONTH.	1879. Temperature. Max.	Min.	Mean.	Rainfall.	1880. Temperature. Max.	Min.	Mean.	Rainfall.	1881. Temperature. Max.	Min.	Mean.	Rainfall.
January.........	.....	.....	.....	.....	59	18	*	.33	49	5	*	4.46
February........	.....	..	.....	.....	48	14	.....	.20	63	18	.....	4.33
March...........	.....	.....	.....	.....	68	12	.....	.29	77	28	.....	.49
April............	.....	.....	.....	.....	86	30	.....	.59	77	35	.....	2.60
May.............	.....	.....	.....	.....	86	36	.....	1.59	88	35	.....	.23
June	.....	.....	.....	.....	93	43	.....	1.07	93	47	.....	2.30
July	.....	.....	.....	.....	100	48	.....	1.87	103	48	72.3	.89
August.........	.....	.....	.....	.....	94	46	.. ..	1.09	100	47	68.9	.31
September.....	.....	.....	.....	.....	92	38	.....	.20	87	37	59.9	1.37
October . .	.....	.....	.....	.....	81	29	.....	1.54	67	28	48.0	1.52
November.....	48	21	.....	.....	62	13	.. ..	2.33	61	18	39.1	1.19
December.....	48	16	.....	.....	54	6	.....	6.31	.....	..	.....	.....

Total rainfall...17.41   Eleven mos......19.74

* No observations of mean temperature taken.   † 8 days.

ALMOTA, WASHINGTON TERRITORY.

Observations commenced April 1, 1881.

April .... 75 Max. 34 Min. 1.65 Rainfall.   August....... 99 Max. 42 Min. .14 Rainfall.
May .... 87 " 33 " .60 "   September.... 90 " 36 " 2.17 "
June.......... 90 " 48 " .70 "   October....... 72 " 26 " 1.95 "
July.... ....103 " 51 " .79 "   November.... 62 " 18 " 1.20 "

COLFAX, WASHINGTON TERRITORY.

Observations commenced Feb. 1, 1881.

February.................. 51 Max. 2 Min.   July .... 99 Max. 37 Min.
March..................... 85 " 26 "   August .... 74 " 35 "
April .... 77 " 22 "   September................. 87 " 27 "
May .... 23 " 25 "   October................... 62 " 17 "
June.................... 91 " 40 "   November................. 55 " 05 "

Astoria, Oregon, latitude, 46° 17' N.; longitude, 123° 50' W. Mean temperature for ten years: Spring, 51° 16'; summer, 61° 30'; autumn, 53° 55'; winter, 42° 43'; for the year, 52° 13'. Annual rainfall, 60 to 67 inches.

Corvallis, Oregon, latitude, 44° 35' N.; longitude, 123° 8' W. Mean temperature for ten years: Spring, 52° 17'; summer, 67° 13'; autumn, 52° 41'; winter, 39° 27'; for the year, 53°. Annual rainfall, 38.47 to 42.08 inches.

For the purpose of comparing the aggregate annual rainfall at Portland and other places in Oregon and Washington Territory with that of many points in various parts of the United States, the following statement from the office of the Chief Signal Officer of the Army is presented. It will be observed that the rainfall at Boston, on the Atlantic seaboard, is only two or three inches lower than that of Portland in the course of the year, and that many other cities east of the Rocky Mountains are so close to the Portland figures, that the difference is not material.

STATEMENT SHOWING THE AVERAGE ANNUAL PRECIPITATION, IN INCHES AND HUNDREDTHS, AT THE STATIONS OF OBSERVATION OF THE SIGNAL SERVICE, UNITED STATES ARMY, NAMED BELOW.

Computed from the Records on File at the Office of the Chief Signal Officer, U. S. Army, Washington, D. C.

STATION.	STATE OR TERRITORY.	AVERAGE ANNUAL RAINFALL.	STATION.	STATE OR TERRITORY.	AVERAGE ANNUAL RAINFALL.	STATION.	STATE OR TERRITORY.	AVERAGE ANNUAL RAINFALL.
Albany	New York	38.75	Dubuque	Iowa	37.93	Milwaukee	Wisconsin	34.31
Alpena	Michigan	36.76	Duluth	Minnesota	33.92	North Platte	Nebraska	18.14
Baltimore	Maryland	42.40	Escanaba	Michigan	38.85	Omaha	Nebraska	33.05
Bismarck	Dakota	23.13	Fort Bennett	Dakota	20.34	Pembina	Dakota	22.21
Boise City	Idaho	12.83	Fort Benton	Montana	15.21	Port Huron	Michigan	34.60
Boston	Massachusetts	49.47	Fort Buford	Dakota	23.25	Sacramento	California	23.94
Breckenridge	Minnesota	25.35	Fort Custer	Montana	19.65	Salt Lake City	Utah	17.52
Cheyenne	Wyoming	10.08	Fort Keogh	Montana	19.89	San Diego	California	10.01
Chicago	Illinois	35.47	Fort Shaw	Montana	13.99	Sandusky	Ohio	40.02
Cleveland	Ohio	38.39	Fort Stevenson	Dakota	16.97	San Francisco	California	23.96
Columbus	Ohio	37.97	Grand Haven	Michigan	39.51	Toledo	Ohio	31.33
Davenport	Iowa	35.80	Helena	Montana	24.20	Visalia	California	10.46
Deadwood	Dakota	23.85	Keokuk	Iowa	38.16	Winnemucca	Nevada	7.21
Denver	Colorado	14.77	La Crosse	Wisconsin	33.72	Yankton	Dakota	27.31
Des Moines	Iowa	34.71	Madison	Wisconsin	40.97	Philadelphia	Pennsylvania	41.89
Detroit	Michigan	35.12	Marquette	Michigan	31.24	Lynchburg	Virginia	41.52

GO TO THE PACIFIC

Which Offers Rich Lands, Healthy Cli
And PROSPERITY

The Northern Pacific Railroad Company,
Oregon Railway and Navigation Company,
AND
Oregon and California Railroad Company

Operate over **4,000** Miles of Transportation by

OCEAN, RIVER and RAIL,

Furnishing UNEQUALED FACILITIES in their magnificent fleet of Ocean and
River Palace Steamboats and Cars to reach all points along the
famous Willamette, picturesque Columbia and Snake
Rivers, and the rich agricultural lands of
Oregon, Washington and Idaho,
now being rapidly settled.

Every few days one of their Steamships—either the "Queen of the Pacific,"
"Columbia," "Oregon," "State of California," "George W.
Elder," or "City of Chester," leaves at 10 A. M.

—From SAN FRANCISCO to PORTLAND, Oregon,—

And returning leaves Portland for San Francisco at 12.05 A. M.

Cars and Steamboats leave Portland for THE DALLES, UMATILLA, WALLA
WALLA, AINSWORTH, CHENEY, SPOKANE FALLS, LAKE PEND D'OREILLE and points
in WESTERN MONTANA, at 7 A. M., every day (Sundays excepted).

ASTORIA, KALAMA, TACOMA and SEATTLE, at 6 A. M., every day (Sundays
excepted).

VICTORIA and NEW WESTMINSTER, 6 A. M., Mondays, Wednesdays and Fridays.

CATHLAMET, BAY VIEW, SKAMOCKAWAY, BROOKFIELD, 6 A. M., Mondays,
Wednesdays and Fridays.

WESTPORT, CLIFTON and KNAPPA, 6 A.M., Tuesdays, Thursdays & Saturdays.

OREGON CITY, SALEM, ALBANY, EUGENE, OAKLAND, ROSEBURG, JACKSONVILLE,
HILLSBORO, FOREST GROVE, YAMHILL, INDEPENDENCE and CORVALLIS, every day
(Sundays excepted).

☞ THROUGH TICKETS at reduced rates over our lines from Portland
to ALL POINTS IN THE EAST.

General Offices—cor. Front and "D" Streets.

C. H. PRESCOTT, *Manager O. R. & N. Co.*
J. W. SPRAGUE, *Gen. Supt. Pacific Div. N. P. R. R., New Tacoma, W. T.*
R. KOEHLER, *Manager O. & C. R. R. Co., Portland, Oregon.*
JOHN MUIR, *Superintendent of Traffic, Portland, Oregon.*
P. SCHULZE, *General Immigration Agent, Portland, Oregon.*
A. L. STOKES, *General Eastern Passenger Agent, 52 Clark Street, Chicago.*
A. ROEDELHEIMER, *General European Agent, 20 Water St., Liverpool, England.*

Printed in the USA
CPSIA information can be obtained
at www.ICGtesting.com
LVHW052251250724
786561LV00030B/777